# Catholic and Married
## Leaning Into Love

# Catholic
## and
# *Married*

### Leaning Into *love*

Art and Laraine Bennett, Editors

Our Sunday Visitor Publishing Division
Our Sunday Visitor, Inc.
Huntington, Indiana 46750

# Contents

# Foreword

By Tom and Karen Edmisten

The winsome bride, Buttercup, sports a look of steely resolve, and Prince Humperdinck, the groom, is solemn. Candles flicker through the majestic church, and organ music pulses over all gathered for the nuptials. The priest, named only "The Impressive Clergyman" in the credits of the movie *The Princess Bride*, looks pointedly at the couple before he opens his mouth to address them and the congregation.

What spills out is wholly incongruous with what has come before: "Mawwiage," he says, "mawwiage is what bwings us togevver today. Mawwiage — that bwessed arrangement, that dweam within a dweam...."

Of course, he wasn't really impressive at all. The wedding over which he was presiding was a sham, and we were rooting for Westley to show up and whisk Buttercup away before she was condemned to a life with that dreadful prince. But the quote prompts laughter and has become a part of our cultural lexicon for a reason. When the clergyman opens his mouth, we expect solemnity befitting the occasion. A little dignity, please, because marriage is serious business.

Whether we are extolling, considering, longing for, celebrating, worrying about, looking forward to, or thanking God for it, marriage indeed brings us together in myriad ways. Everyone loves weddings, big parties, bestowing gifts. We love falling in love. We anticipate nuptials, our own or others', with giddy hope, happiness, best wishes, and prayers for the lucky couple. We hold fast to ideals about the fairy tale wedding, the perfect marriage, charming children. In short, we want to live "Happily Ever After."

"Ever After," however, isn't happy all the time — we all know about that pesky thing called Reality — but it isn't a castle in the air either. There *is* a place called Happily Ever After. Marriage — invented, patented, and marketed by God — can be all that it's cracked up to be. The "Happily Ever After" of marriage is doable, and not *just* doable, but incredible, and far more common than the world would have us think. Wedded bliss dishes out some of the best stuff life has to offer: surprises, joy, exponentially expansive love. Marriage is not something we simply make the best of as we trudge through the days after the fairy-tale wedding. Marriage *is* the best.

## Surprised by Joy

Before you accuse of us being Pollyannas, let us confess a little messiness. We haven't always held marriage in such high regard. When we first decided to make a life together, we did not head straight to the altar. Honestly? We deliberately avoided that path. An atheist (Karen) and a lapsed Lutheran (Tom), we lived together for three years before we decided, "What the heck, we may as well get married, huh?" We planned our wedding in three weeks to make it coincide with a weekend Karen's parents would be in town for a visit. We called a judge, made an appointment, bought a couple of wedding bands, and booked a room at a restaurant for dinner.

Bam! We were married.

So, we caved on one traditional value that we'd planned to forego, but we remained steadfast in our position on children. We didn't want 'em. No reason to give in to every bit of traditional madness, right? We were reinventing marriage in our own image.

It wasn't until Karen's conversion to Christianity that she perceived a larger purpose to marriage and began entertaining the possibility of a family. Tom wasn't convinced. But as the desire for a baby grew more important to Karen, he eventually came on board. We stopped using birth control, promptly got pregnant, just as promptly lost two babies to miscarriage, and finally had our first daughter, Emily.

About eighteen months after Emily came along, so did Karen's conversion to Catholicism. Tom wanted nothing to do with *that*, but out of love and respect for Karen he agreed not to stand in her way, and to live without artificial birth control. We had our second daughter, Lizzy, and three more heartbreaking miscarriages. Then came another conversion: Tom was received into the Catholic Church five years after Karen. And just when we thought God didn't want us to have any more children, our third daughter, Kate, was born.

The atheist and the lapsed Lutheran who'd married on a whim and vowed to remain child-free were now a Catholic couple with three daughters on earth and a bunch of kids in heaven. That's a lot of changes for two people who initially thought living together and ignoring God would be just fine.

We were no longer the people we'd been sixteen years before when we stood in front of a judge and said, "I do." It wasn't merely the passage of time and the adoption of religion that had changed us. Marriage changed us. Marriage shaped us, challenged us, formed us, and defined us. It helped us to grow up and grow together. These two became one.

# A Job vs. a Career

We often hear that marriage is work. We get tired of that idea. Don't you? It's more accurate to say that marriage exacts effort, as do all great works of art. Energy put forth in a worthwhile endeavor *could* be called "work," but it rings truer to say that nurturing a marriage is a privilege, an honor, and — you hear this less often, but it's true — a lot of fun. It's the difference between punching a clock for a weekly paycheck and investing your time in a meaningful career that you love.

Let's look at it another way. In other areas of life we don't call exhilarating, energy-expending activities "work." We rarely belittle delightful hobbies by labeling them drudgery. Imagine saying this: "I love to (fill in the blank: garden/ hike/ski/run/golf/read/swim/work on cars/write/teach/play football/bake/play guitar), but boy is it *work*!" We don't qualify our passions as if the sweat negated the fruits. We love the sweat as much as the result, the satisfaction, and the accomplishment. So it goes with marriage. Effort? Yes. Worth it? Yes.

In Mindy Kaling's *Is Everyone Hanging Out Without Me?*, Kaling, who is not a Catholic, has a sweet, optimistic, hopeful view of marriage. It's a view so simple and true that it strikes us as fully Catholic in its way. Kaling also gets tired of people saying marriage is work: "I guess I think happiness can come in a bunch of forms, and maybe a marriage with tons of work makes people happy. But part of me still thinks … is it really so hard to make it work? What happened to being pals?… Maybe the point is that any marriage is work, but you may as well pick work that you like."

Yes. Exactly. Pick work that you like. Pick a person you like, too.

# Six Little Words

Pope Francis summed up the makings of a healthy marriage when he said that successful family life relies on turning often to these three phrases: "May I? Thank you. I'm sorry."

This sounds oppressive, as if we must walk on eggshells in our love nests, always asking permission, straining at formal niceties, apologizing for every microscopic transgression. But the simple courtesy of "May I?" means we don't presume, even of those we love most, that we have an unfettered right to everything we want. "Thank you" can never be exhausted, since gratitude keeps love and morale afloat. And real love is being willing to say, "I'm sorry," as often as necessary, whether seven times, or seventy-times-seven.

We see these realities play out daily in our own marriage and can attest to the power of the pope's words. Karen doesn't need permission to socialize, but framing it this way: "Do you mind if I head out for coffee tonight with my friends?" is a courteous acknowledgement that Tom might have plans she is unaware of. When Tom says, "Have I thanked you for all that laundry you did today?" it's lovely to have what's expected feel appreciated. And tiny apologies ("I'm sorry I snapped at you, I think I need more coffee….") add up; they keep the little stuff from turning into big stuff.

## Seasons and Sacraments

Practicing the pope's six little words every day can fortify a marriage for bigger challenges, too. No matter how much we'd like to avoid it, our fallen world imposes stress. Marriages will inevitably go through stages that stretch us. The arrival of a baby or the strain of infertility, children entering school or the start of a homeschool, illness, caring for aging parents, military deployment, job changes, and financial worries are all realities that catapult marriage into untrod territory, leaving us feeling that there's no time to explore new ground. We're too busy getting our bearings. It's sad to see a couple split up in the middle of a crisis or an extremely challenging phase of life. *If only they'd waited*, we think. *Now they won't experience the wealth of joy that's waiting on the other side of this season.*

Our wish for couples, including ourselves, is that we will always stand firm on the sacramental foundation God provides. As a sacrament, marriage is an outward sign of an inward grace, and thanks to that reality our part in this relationship is easier. Think about it: God uses marriage as a delivery system for grace. He lets us find someone insanely attractive to us, has us fall in love, lets us drop into bed with this person every night, prompts us to make cute little replicas of ourselves, and on top of all that, we get to have pizza and beer on a regular basis with this gem we call a spouse. Then He uses all this blithesome fun to save our eternal souls and little by little make us holier. Wow. That's kind of crazy and kind of amazing.

## Is That Your Final Answer?

A healthy, faithful, sacramentally fortified marriage is a witness to a world that is aching for happiness. Those with the courage to commit share a profound truth with the world: that there is more to life than acting on our whims and personal desires, that sacrifices offered in love are worth offering — not only because they are right and good, but because, ironically, they bring us the very happiness we seek but fear we'll lose when we give ourselves away.

God created marriage for the long haul. Long hauls, be they bus trips, hikes, or marriages, have their peaks and valleys, and just a few ground rules. Traveling together requires politeness, gratitude, and forgiveness. Muscles of all kinds must be exercised. There will be times we can't wait to get to the next rest stop. There will be breathless treks wherein we can't fathom crossing a river or climbing a mountain without the companion at our side, the one we're holding onto so tightly. There will be memories and great story-telling. And there will be exhilaration when the final destination comes into heart-stopping, glorious view.

Marriage, that blessed arrangement, that dream within a dream, is unpredictable, exciting, thrilling, beautiful, hard, easy, the best of times, the worst of times, massively complicated, and deceptively simple. Do you want to enter into the adventure of a lifetime?

You know the answer to the question: "I do."

---

*Tom and Karen Edmisten, both converts to Catholicism, have been wed long enough to know that marriage is a gift worth unwrapping. Karen is the author of* Deathbed Conversions: Finding Faith at the Finish Line *and* After Miscarriage. *They live with their three daughters in the Midwest.*

Chapter 1

# Mirrors Around a Flame
## The Gift of Children

By Simcha Fisher

When I got pregnant for the first time, things were not going well. The pregnancy itself was fine; it was the rest of my life that was a mess. I was bitter and depressed, hopeless and out of control. I knew that life had meaning for other people, and I knew that I was not doing well, but I couldn't get those gears to mesh. I couldn't get myself to do right. I couldn't persuade myself that living was worth the effort — that my life was worth the effort. It was easier, so much easier, to keep on drifting and suffering.

When the pregnancy test turned up positive, I made a few changes right away: no more smoking, much less drinking. But otherwise, I stayed the same. I knew in theory that my life was changing in a big way, but I didn't feel it.

Then one day, about a week into my pregnancy, a casual f-bomb slipped past my lips. And it hung there in the air, sounding stupid and foul and poisonous. It sounded like a bomb for real, with the sickening thud and that dreadful ripping sound as the air is torn apart. I had never heard a word sound so ugly before, so disastrous. It sounded that way because I had said it in front of my baby, my little one, this being who was, according to the books, the size of a grain of rice.

What was the big deal? She couldn't understand me, or even hear me. She didn't even have ears yet. But I was in the presence of someone who had never had any experience of ugliness of any kind. And I did not want — with my whole heart, I did *not* want — to be the one who started her out on that education.

That was when things began to change. It's not that I stopped swearing on that day. And it's not that I immediately went squeaky clean, or made a solemn vow to look on the sunny side. Sixteen years later, I'm still knee deep in the clean-up operation of my life — still figuring out which of my habits are harmless, which are helpful, and which ones really need to go.

But I'll never forget that day, when I realized, aghast and amazed, that I had some choices to make. It was about more than whether or not I wanted to teach my kids to swear. I had to face the question of which side I wanted to be on. I knew beyond all doubt that there was still innocence in the world. For the first time, it was very clear that what I do and what I say either helps protect that innocence, or helps defile it. There could be no drifting any more. I had to choose. Do I want to make things better, or worse?

This was the first gift I received when I had my child: the gift of hearing myself, of coming to myself. I was jarred out of a string of random, senseless, casual, habitual words and actions. What I said and did mattered. I mattered.

You may say, "I don't need a baby to tell me that! I already know that I matter." And maybe you do. Maybe your life is not a mess, as mine was. But most modern people have one thing in common: we need help launching from knowledge to action. We need something urgent to propel us from potential into effort. We need to reach a defining moment, when good and evil become real to us — when our choices become real. And nothing does this like a child, a new little person who is waiting to be taught.

Children want to know, even before they are born: What is the world like? Is life good or bad? And you will want to give them the right answer, even if you have to change your ways to make that answer true. Changing will be a pleasure.

Is life good, they will ask? Maybe it's not good enough, not yet. But now that you are here, little one, we will move heaven and earth to make it better for you.

## What Kind of Gift Is a Child?

The *Catechism of the Catholic Church* says that children are "the supreme gift of marriage [who] contribute greatly to the good of the parents themselves" (1652). What kind of gift? The gift of giving us a reason to change, to repent, to see right and wrong clearly, and to choose.

Some gift, right? It sounds like the kind of gift that demands things from the receiver. It sounds a little bit like something a celibate man would be enthusiastic about, because it's a good theory! "Just accept this gift, and your life will be great! I'm going back to my nice, quiet rectory now." But in practice, children give us burdens and responsibilities, don't they?

Well, of course. When you have children, your life will be changed forever. It will be harder to do whatever you want, and every decision you make will be tethered by the consideration of how it will affect your children. Once you have children, your marriage will never be the same.

And you will praise God for it. You will never regret this life of joys and sorrows, frustrations and exaltations, petty duties and profound revelations. You will, as it says in the rite of Baptism, thank God for the gift of your child.

Let's get specific. What do children do for us, besides wreck our bodies, steal our sleep, cost us money, and turn our hair grey? How are they gifts to our marriage, specifically — so much so that one of the primary purposes of marriage is to bear and raise children?

Let's look at the idea of a gift in general — just a literal gift, with wrapping paper and ribbons. Read any advice column and you'll see that the world is full of people who have no idea what gifts are all about. They behave as if gifts are something they are entitled to — and if they don't get what they feel they deserve, down to the tiniest detail, they don't care who they hurt while they rearrange things to their liking. And they never say, "Thank you."

If this is how people treat material gifts that come in a box, it should come as no surprise that, for many people, the concept of children as *gifts* is not so compelling. Theirs is a more self-absorbed, pragmatic approach to gifts. This is why we have nightmarish dilemmas like, "My husband doesn't want to pay the fees to store our excess frozen embryos. Should I insist?" Or, "I told my fiancé that I'm tired of this visitation nonsense, and he needs to choose between me and his kids."

This utilitarian attitude is why there are horrors like the child sex slave trade: children are treated as property — useful as long as we want them, worthless as soon as we don't.

Since children are valued according to how much satisfaction they can supply, it's no surprise that many couples opt out altogether. Raising children is hard work. They put heavy demands on a couple's time, attention, and finances; and even with the help of technology, there's no way to guarantee that heartache and suffering won't come our way. Why bother? Why not keep things simple — just you and me, work and play, do our best, then fade away?

I'll tell you why. Because if a married couple voluntarily opts out of children — if you decide you're just going to skip it, because they're a hassle, and they're scary, and they're expensive and messy and will make you work hard, and will *change* you — then you're depriving yourself of a joy that I can't even hope to describe.

There is nothing like children. Not pets, not hobbies, not careers. There is no love like the love for children. It draws spouses together and increases their capacity to love each other. It draws us closer to God, and makes us more fully human. Love for children enriches the world and gives life meaning. It gives us purpose and strength. Love for children teaches us something that is central to every good man's and every good woman's understanding of life: that there is good, and there is bad, and that we are here to make a choice.

## The Gifts Children Offer to a Married Couple

*Children make you remember, over and over,*
*the basic truths you need to hear.*

Just today at Mass, my four-year-old asked me, "Why are we kneeling?" At that very moment, an honest answer would have been, "Because everybody else is kneeling, honey. Now hush, so I can get back to thinking about my hair." But she needed a better answer than that, so I told her, "We're kneeling because we're here to worship God. He came down from heaven to be with us, so we're kneeling down because He's so good, and we're so glad He's here." And thank you for the reminder, my dear. I needed it.

*Children make us think hard about questions
we never did figure out the first time around.*

What's the real difference between girls and boys? Why are we here? What happens after we die? We can go through our whole lives dodging these questions, but our kids will ask (and will reject anything that sounds phony). We adults need a good answer just as much as they do.

*Children are funny.*

Sounds trivial, doesn't it? It's not. The world is cold and hard. Children, with their silliness and sweet nuttiness, bring us steady doses of innocent joy, with no irony, no guilt, no nastiness. One day, my little son approached, his curly head held unnaturally still. "Pea-yuck," he confided, "on mine heg!" For the first time in my life, I rejoiced to see someone with peanuts on his head — and years later, I still laugh every time I remember it. It's the pleasure of simple happiness, something that everyone needs — and it comes to parents many times every single day.

*Children draw parents together and magnify
the love they  have for each other.*

Two people often become friends because they love the same thing — baseball, education, knitting, antique engines. Now imagine what happens between two people who love the same *person* — a person they made or brought into their family together. Love begets love. Becoming parents is like holding up mirrors around a flame.

I fell in love with my husband because I liked his ways, I liked his looks, I liked the way he dealt with the world, and I'd rather be with him than with anyone else. Every child we have together has something of this man in him: the shape of his eyebrows, the cleft in his chin, his posture, the way his mind works — with fascinating additions and permutations of their own. More to love!

*Children make life orderly.*

Not in the way that you think! My house, which is full of children, is only about as orderly as the inside of a wind tunnel. But I'm not talking about overcoming that kind of disorder. I'm talking about the kind of disorder that pushes an old woman to smear her face with makeup and struggle into a push-up bra, because being sexy is the only virtue she knows. I'm talking about the disorder that makes grown men sniff after teenage girls, because all they can see is what they want, and not where they are, or who they are supposed to be.

When your childbearing years are centered on raising children together with your spouse, and preparing them to leave you and to start their own families, you can shrug all that foolishness off, because it so clearly doesn't make sense. Your life as parents may be untidy in details, but it has a clear design.

*Children remind us that we are going to die.*

Sounds like a lovely gift, doesn't it? But it's one we need. We all know someone who doesn't seem to know that life has time limits — someone who behaves as if all choices are still in the nebulous future. Children come with a very clear time stamp — one we are forced to acknowledge when we pack away the outgrown dinosaur PJs. Or when we realize that the brochure from a college isn't junk mail, but is intended for our children, who are almost done being children. They make us achingly aware that time is fleeting, and that we had better concentrate our efforts on the kind of behavior that will stand up well in eternity.

*Children rescue you from selfishness and teach you
that the whole world is a child.*

Do freedom and contentment come from getting what you
want? Nope. Not for long, anyway. Do not be deceived:
people who get what they want all the time are in a prison,
and every time they get their own way, they're building
the walls higher. There is something more liberating than
getting what you want, and that's realizing that you can do
without, and still be happy; that you can give, and be even
happier.

Before I had kids, I liked them well enough, but their
problems were more like case studies than like an out-
stretched hand. Now that I've had so many little ones depending on me, it's impossible for me to look away from
someone — child or adult — who needs help. I can't help
everyone, and I'm not always in the mood to do it, but at
the very least I understand that it is my job to help if I can.
It's what I'm here for.

There are enough cool-headed observers in the world.
What we need is more people who are willing to guide, help,
protect, defend, and feed.

*Children teach you that you are helpless.*

It is very easy to imagine that we are in control of our lives.
When things are going well, it's hard to resist the illusion
that things will continue to go well as long as we continue to
make good choices, perfectly calibrated with the right pro-
portions of prudence, courage, and integrity.

Enter a toddler, or a teenager, or a grown child, and
suddenly you see very clearly that you are not in control, and
that you need God desperately. You think your house was
childproofed, until a clever child learns, while you are asleep,

how to get into the attic, and you wake to see her hurtling headfirst through the trapdoor in your bedroom ceiling. You remember mending stuffed bunnies, baking muffins, and singing lullabies; your teenager remembers broken promises, guilt trips, and unjust punishments.

And it's all true: you did your best, and you still failed. You are still beloved by God. Everyone needs grace and mercy; not everyone realizes it.

*Children teach us to be grateful.*

Once we form the habit of turning to God in our need, we will learn to turn to Him in our joy also, giving Him praise for the things that go well — whether because of, or in spite of, our efforts. When we turn our bad days over to God, He blunts their pain; when we turn our good ones over to Him, He magnifies their pleasure.

*Children give us a second chance at building the parent-child relationship.*

When you and your spouse talk about the way you were raised, you will probably remember some good and some bad — some things you can only hope to replicate with your own children (reading Dickens on Christmas Eve) and some things you would rather die than pass along to another generation (almost nonexistent sex education). Nothing exorcises painful childhood memories like doing it right with your own kids; and no pleasures are warmer than building on happy memories by writing the next chapter with your own children.

Hashing out your hopes and fears with your spouse will also help you to understand each other. There is nothing like a good origin story to build sympathy; and sympathy is essential in marriage.

*Children highlight your spouse's
strengths and talents.*

Five or six times a week, I mutter at my kids, "And *that's* why you have two parents." Sometimes the kid is a wailing toddler who is having mysterious trouble with her sleeping bag, and my husband brings forth secret reserves of patience and tenderness — and I adore him for it. Other times the kid is a struggling student who needs help with homework, and I discover that I once read a book on this very topic — and my husband admires me for it.

Little seedlings of virtue and talent come into full bloom when children need us, and our spouses find more to love when they see us in blossom.

*Children give us a reason to keep
our marriages strong.*

It's fashionable to scoff at benighted old couples who used to stay together for the sake of the children. Now that it's common to seek a no-fault divorce over problems such as boredom or irritation, it's also become more socially acceptable to talk honestly about how divorce fragments the lives of the children involved. Sometimes divorce is necessary, but more often it isn't.

Children give us a reason to work hard at making our marriage better. They give us the strength to pick up the cross of marriage over and over again — because we know the children are watching, because we know they're learning, because they need to see that struggles can be overcome. And because they need both of us. They need unity.

*Children give our bodies purpose.*

I always have to laugh when people complain, "The Church treats women like baby-making machines!" The truth is, the secular world is the one that treats women that way — and expends tremendous amounts of money and effort in trying to find the "off" button, often putting women through years of physical and psychological contortions with one kind of contraception after another.

The Church, on the other hand, teaches that the bodies of men and women are designed the way they are, reproductive systems and all, because they have a specific purpose in life. What is that purpose? Something huge: to make love, literally. To create something, to bring new love into the world. Sometimes this looks like physically bearing children (whether many or few); sometimes it looks like adopting; sometimes it looks like simply becoming aware that we are all here to love and to be loved.

When my first baby was born, someone in the delivery room asked, "Is it a boy or a girl?" and I thought to myself, "Holy mackerel, it's a *baby*!" Human anatomy class told me this was normal and mundane — the natural product of sex. But the wrinkled face, the velvety shoulders, the deep dark eyes of my newborn daughter — this was the product of love. Our bodies, our love, had made her. Fifteen years later, we're still amazed.

*Children are the ultimate opportunity*
*to give back to society.*

We hear so often about children being a drain on society, either because they have special needs that require expensive care, or just because, being human, they eat food and drink water and wear clothes and take up space. Couples feel as if they have to justify or apologize for giving birth to more than a replacement number of children.

Can we remember, for a moment, where people come from? What is society made up of? Former children. Architects, scientists, teachers, musicians, plumbers, anyone you admire, anyone you depend on — someone decided to bring that person into the world. It's crazy to even have to say so, but somebody really does have to be the one to have children! The world needs people.

*Children teach us how it's possible to love someone without approving of their behavior.*

This idea is central to the Gospel: Christ loved us enough to come into the world *because* He does not approve of our behavior — because He, in His love for us, knew that we needed to be rescued, guided, corrected, saved. He teaches us to love the sinner, hate the sin. Parents don't stop loving their child when he runs into the road, skips school, or drifts into drugs. It's because they love him that they want him to change.

*Children teach us how God must see us.*

Perhaps we imagine that God is a spoilsport or a control freak — that He calls all the fun stuff "sin" just to jerk us around. We are cured of this foolish idea the very first time we say "no" to a child who wants to eat motor oil or dance on the edge of the Grand Canyon. We save their lives by telling them no, and how do they repay us? By crying, by screaming, by telling us we're mean. Sound familiar? Parents say "no" to their children because they love them and want to protect them. God does the same for us.

~

There you have it: a short, surface-skimming introduction to the value of children.

And yet, there are parents in the world who do not consider their children to be gifts. Heck, sometimes my husband and I *are* those parents. Sometimes we treat our kids like hassles, like expensive and messy and scary interferences in our time, in our *real* lives. But that's the thing about a gift: it's something freely given, and the recipient really is free to do whatever he likes with it. He can squander it. He can be ungrateful. He can complain, and protest, and not take proper care of it. He can utterly fail to realize what a precious thing he has received, if that's what he wants to do.

Children don't fail-proof your marriage or your life. While they can be a source of daily joy and satisfaction, they don't provide a guarantee of any kind. They do not compel, but they invite. They have the power to bring out the best in us — not one time, but over and over again.

Remember that grain of rice, and how that tiny, unformed person I was sheltering brought me to myself? That was not a one-time deal. That choice, that invitation, happens again and again, as we live our lives with our children and realize beyond all doubt that we matter, that what we do matters, and that we want to be on the side of good.

What a gift.

---

*Simcha Fisher is the author of* The Sinners Guide to Natural Family Planning. *She is a speaker and freelance writer, and she blogs for Patheos at* I Have to Sit Down *and for the* National Catholic Register. *She, her husband, Damien, and their children live in New Hampshire.*

Chapter 2

# *Trending Toward Joy*
## *Taking the Long View*

By Art and Laraine Bennett

It's 1945 and post-war Vienna is a gritty scene of espionage, black market intrigue, and Russian soldiers terrorizing the streets. Laraine's mom, a German artist, is now working for the Americans. One day, as she tells it, a strikingly handsome, curly-haired officer comes striding in from the field. She takes one look at him and knows: this is the man I am going to marry. Their romance lasted sixty-three years until God called the highly decorated World War II and Korean War veteran home.

This marriage — and others like it — give all of us hope because their marriage was not a matter of long-suffering endurance, teeth-gritting stick-to-it-ness, or spiteful perseverance. This was a Christian marriage to aspire to: transformational love, true happiness, a unity of two unique individuals that — mysteriously — is even better than either of the two alone.

Of course they had their share of trouble, as all of us do, but still we wonder: is this even possible? A marriage that is a happy adventure of two-become-one? Where neither person loses his individuality, where one person is not subsumed into the other nor crushed under the power of the other but, rather, becomes his better self, his true self? Where the two only reach their "master speed" as the poet Robert Frost wrote, when they are forever united "wing to wing and oar to oar"?

## Our Journey Begins

We were married during Spring Break, not a particularly auspicious beginning for a lifetime sacramental marriage covenant. But we were in graduate school, in a beach town in California (that may explain everything), and we wanted our friends and classmates to be able to join with us in the festivities.

Our dear friend and philosophy professor, Fr. Timothy Fallon, S.J., drove down from Northern California to the small campus church where nobody had ever been married before — because, hello, this is the seventies in Santa Barbara!

Nonetheless, by the grace of God, we have been married now for thirty-six years. And we've been blessed. We've had our hurdles and our bumps in the road, but we have been spared some of the major sufferings that others we know have experienced: job loss, homelessness, major illness, addictions, abuse, and affairs. On the other hand, of course, one might compare the slow drip-drip-drip of married life to a kind of "white" martyrdom.

Several years after our wedding we were still living in expensive, crunchy California, but now we had two small children and jobs that barely covered our living expenses. Laraine was a freelance writer for textbook publishers, writing advertising copy, and Art was just starting out as a marriage and family therapist. We rented a seven hundred-square-foot duplex on the "wrong" side of Palo Alto. Laraine would sell an occasional valued philosophy book at the local used book store to get money for lattes. We did the math and realized that we were never going to be able to afford to buy a house. So we were open for change. This change happened by way of neighbors, also in the business of psychology, also with two small children, who were looking into working overseas helping military families dealing with substance abuse.

Uprooting our family, moving seven thousand miles away to a country where we didn't speak (or just barely spoke) the language, living in the middle of an entirely different culture was the turning point of our lives.

Up until now, our faith had been somewhat lukewarm. We were pretty much the average pew-sitters: attending Mass on Sundays, giving up chocolate during Lent, baptizing our kids.

Now we were strangers in a strange land, wayfarers with a baby and a three-year-old. Germans (at the time already well below the replacement birth rate) stared at us, incredulous: the baby crawling through the dirty train corridors, four noisy Americans schlepping diaper bags, Cheerios, and children through the pristine German countryside. One woman, horrified, exclaimed, "You look like third-world refugees!" German grandmothers pointed and told us that the baby's legs were exposed; waiters informed us that babies and small children were not allowed (dogs only), and we were stranded in the Army hotel, unable to find a place to live.

The American chaplain told us that, as part of the Catholic community, we cannot be pew-sitters. No more anonymity, no more quick escape as soon as Mass is over. Each one of us must be involved. He tasked Art with leading a Baptism class, Laraine with CCD, and said that we will tithe 10 percent. Also, each Sunday after Mass we will go with him on a Volksmarch — Americans and Germans hiking together for hours through alpine forests and meadows, stopping occasionally for a refreshing beer! We were now responsible for one another, we were part of a larger community, we were given a mission.

And in a certain sense, our marriage unfolded from there.

## But First, the Perspective of Temperament

Happy couples, as Art has learned in his clinical practice and his study of psychology, are continually working on their relationship and growing as a team. They don't take each other for granted, slogging away for thirty or forty years, losing themselves in career or children, and then waking up one day to an empty nest and a stranger in their bed. Certainly, there will be times when it's all about gritting your teeth and enduring the pain. But overall, the trend of happy couples is toward joy, especially finding the joy in the present moment.

Sometimes, the present moment is exceedingly difficult. We recall vividly those sleepless nights with a brand-new colicky baby and those anxiety-ridden days in a foreign country when we feared we would never find a place to live. Yet through it all we somehow kept seeking the joy: whether it was learning to ask for advice or laughing bemusedly when we were chastised for the racket our kids created on their noisy "big wheels" during German "quiet time."

Even when we love someone dearly, however, we sometimes say or do the wrong thing. How we express ourselves can encourage further discussion — or start a fight. Many factors contribute to the way we handle situations, but our temperament has a lot do with how intensely we feel things, whether or not we express our feelings, and how we communicate. Understanding temperament can help provide perspective and context as a couple moves forward in their marriage.[1]

Before Laraine learned about the concept of temperament, she used to think Art was just like her ... only bad. When he didn't want to talk about something immediately, she assumed he was being "distant," or even anti-social. Her willingness — even exuberance — to discuss a point (read: argue) left him frustrated. So there were many occasions, especially during those particularly stressful times, when Laraine would assume that Art was purposefully neglecting her, and she would redouble her efforts to engage — by arguing, confronting, and challenging — which only served to push introverted Art further into his shell.

Some people find it easy to express their innermost thoughts and feelings, while others are more reserved. Still others are impulsive, and say the first thing that pops into their heads — which may be less than tactful. Some people react quickly and strongly (and come down like a sledge hammer). Others react slowly, more tentatively. These are differences in temperament.

Many arguments and feelings of frustration can be dissolved like fog in the afternoon sun when we discover that spouses are often suffering simply under the burden of not knowing their own temperament and its foibles. Your spouse is not doing "mean things" to you "on purpose," nor is he trying to start a fight or punish you. Rather, he acts like that or talks like that (or doesn't talk) because of his God-given temperament.

Once we began studying temperament seriously, we became even more convinced that our own extremely opposite reactions should not be fodder fueling fights, but rather, should become occasions for laughter and compromise. What really matters in a marriage is agreement on core values; that one prefers reading and solitude while the other gravitates to shopping and socializing are less foundational.

Temperament is helpful, but it's only part of the package that helps couples become secure in their marriage. Successful couples — having grown older and wiser (and sometimes grumpier) and having picked up some annoying tics and some bad habits along the way — work on bettering themselves humanly and spiritually. With the grace from the sacraments — and sometimes help from counseling professionals — they grow stronger as individuals and as a couple, keeping their relationship healthy.

## Three Pillars of a Healthy Marriage

In Art's extensive work with Catholic couples and families over the past thirty years, he has identified three pillars that are foundational to strong, lasting marriages:

- healthy communication;

- a willingness to forgive;

- and, most important, the grace from the sacrament of marriage and from an ongoing participation in the sacraments of the Church.

These might seem self-evident, but any marriage can hit rocky times when communication or forgiveness or even the life of faith can seem lost. Even strong sacramental marriages can face a "dark night of the soul" of the marriage. It may be addiction, depression, temptations from without, or the cross from within, but whatever the source, it is truly a dark night. Couples who establish these three pillars in their marriage — and the sooner the better — will have a much stronger ability to handle the challenges that come their way.

## Communication: Keeping the Drawbridge Down

Jesus tells us that in marriage "the two shall become one" (Matthew 19:5). What kind of unity is this? We've seen marriages where this supposed unity is merely the tyrannical imposition of one partner's rule over the other. Or marriages in which the unity exists in name only. Yet Jesus assures us that it is possible, and experience tells us that communication is key.

Talking about communication always seems somewhat superficial or trite. Nonetheless, as one wise priest tells engaged couples, marriage *is* communication, in the deepest sense. But it is not so helpful to say: "Just do it." It is more useful to provide a few tried and true principles of good communication, so you can have in your back pocket some tips for communicating well. Here are three essential principles that have risen to the surface in Art's counseling work, tips that can be practiced "in season and out of season."

### The Underlying Positive

When we are angry or hurt, we tend to forget about the good things in our life and those things we love about our spouse and focus only on whatever is wrong. Sometimes we let the negative feelings build up or we stifle our complaints for so long that we become submerged under a dark cloud of negativity. When we see the dirty socks on the bathroom floor or the receipt from the mall, we are immediately swamped by negativity: "Why is he always such a slob?" or "She is incapable of sticking to a budget!" Foremost marriage researcher John Gottman calls this "negative sentiment override." We stockpile grievances, keeping track of each and every offense, no matter how small.[2] Everything becomes indicative of our spouse's ill will and bad character. Love cannot possibly thrive in such a poisonous atmosphere. The antidote to this negative sentiment override is expressing the underlying positive.

Expressing the underlying positive eliminates defensiveness by acknowledging the good intentions of your spouse. When you are angry because your spouse has been coming home late every night, missing dinner, leaving you to help the kids with their homework and put them to bed, remembering why this is happening might help you to avoid lashing out.

You don't need to *bury* your feelings, you just need to express them in a positive, loving way, recognizing that he or she is not intentionally trying to ruin your day or make you unhappy.

Here's an illustration of this principle at work in our own marriage. After a ten-year foray into homeschooling, we cast our kids to the four winds and the adventures of various schools. But it soon became clear that getting everyone together for a family dinner was like getting Odysseus home from Troy. We were juggling basketball, swimming, and football practices, science projects, piano lessons, drivers ed, different schools and different friends, along with the daily commute amid the insane traffic of the Washington, DC, area. It was a herculean effort to say the least. When we finally sat down to dinner, it was often 9:00 p.m.

So, these dinners were precious. Melancholic Art decided to capitalize on the moment and became the Emily Post of the household. He critiqued posture, manners, and quality of conversation. Dinners became increasingly tense. Choleric Laraine compensated by arguing with everything. Usually, at least one child (sometimes a parent) would storm away from the dinner table in high dudgeon.

Laraine had recently learned — at Art's urging — some communication techniques, and she decided to try them out. Instead of yelling at Art, "What's the matter with you? You're always so negative! Nobody is going to want to have dinner with you anymore!" she decided to practice her newfound diplomatic skills.

So Laraine invited Art out for a walk. She began with, "I think it's so awesome how you have been trying to get home at a decent hour so we can have a family dinner. I know how difficult your commute is and how demanding your job, yet you have made family time a priority. There is just one thing I'd like to discuss with you, and I think it would make our family time even more fruitful. Let me know when you'd like to talk about it." And we did discuss it (it was a long walk), but Art was neither bombarded by negativity nor was he blindsided by the criticism.

St. John Chrysostom recognized this principle of good communication, though he didn't label it as "the underlying positive." He wrote: "Whenever you give your wife advice, always begin by telling her how much you love her." And, "A wife should never nag her husband: 'You lazy coward, you have no ambition! Look at our relatives and neighbors; they have plenty of money. Their wives have far more than I do.'"[3]

Expressing the underlying positive is not the same as flattering, buttering up, or lying. It means looking at the *bigger picture*, recognizing what is good about your spouse and your situation and acknowledging the good intentions of your beloved. Yes, you may be angry *right now*, but the underlying positive is that you *do* love your spouse, and remain committed in good times and in bad.

Research has shown that acknowledging the good things of your life, even the very small things — counting your blessings — makes people happy. Developing the communication habit of expressing the underlying positive helps infuse your marriage with gratitude and joy. Remember that although Christ healed ten lepers, only one came back to thank him, and to him Jesus says, "Your faith has saved you" (Luke 17:19, NAB).

### Be Empathic

Empathy is a Christ-like putting yourself in another's shoes, seeking to understand before being understood, and removing the beam from your own eye before you try to remove the speck from your spouse's. You listen and respond to your spouse in a way that shows you understand what he is saying and feeling. Instead of immediately rushing in to solve whatever problem you think your spouse has or to rebut whatever point you think he is making, stop. Hit the pause button and make sure you understand what your spouse has been trying to tell you.

Early in our marriage, after we had had our first child, Laraine worked part-time at a publishing company while Art juggled grad school and an internship. Money was extremely tight, we were living in that cramped Palo Alto duplex guarded by a crazy dog that only barked at the residents and never at strangers, and we desperately wanted to improve our situation. Even so, the tug on Laraine's heartstrings grew insistent as she dropped our sensitive toddler, stressed by the disruptions to her schedule, off at the babysitter. Laraine became less and less enamored with "having it all" — a career and motherhood — but we couldn't see how to make this work financially. She finally blurted out to Art the depth of her misery and her desire to quit her job.

Art responded with empathy and said immediately that there had to be some way to make this possible despite the financial instability this would bring, not to mention putting on hold our hope to move into a single-family home. This empathy led the way to finding a creative solution: Laraine became a freelancer working from home, so she could spend time with our small family. Not only did Art's empathy enable the two of us to find a creative solution, but it also brought us closer together.

As Pope Benedict XVI wrote, when we really listen, truly attend to what the other person is trying to say, our "own being is enriched and deepened because it is united with the being of the other."[4] Seeking to understand enhances love. And if something we have done causes negative feelings or stress, when we pause and allow our spouse to say what he feels (even though we may want to jump in with our explanation) we are creating a sacred space in which love can grow. Only after being empathic should you explain, "My cell phone died so I couldn't call," or, "My boss called me in for a surprise meeting."

Empathy is not the same as sympathy. You do not have to *feel* the same way your spouse does! Nonetheless, you are taking up your cross: you must die to yourself and listen to what your spouse is saying and feeling. This is empathy.

### Be Open to Influence

Being open to influence is a *communication habit that requires humility*. Sometimes we refuse to listen to our spouse's thoughts or feelings because we believe that we've heard it all before and we disagree with him. We may fear that allowing the other person to have his or her say is to admit agreement. Yet when we refuse to listen to our spouse, we are betraying an element of pride: our view is the only correct one. If I always insist on having the last word or that things go my way, and dismiss my partner's thoughts and feelings, then I risk being condescending, even contemptuous. And contempt is a marriage poison.

A number of years ago, out of the blue, Art announced that he wanted to go backpacking in the wilderness. You know, the kind where you are dropped by a helicopter on the top of Mount McKinley and you have to find your own way out, guided only by the stars. Laraine immediately snorted (supportively), "That's insane!"

Now, if you knew Art, you would know that Laraine was speaking the truth. The last time we went camping, we couldn't get the coffee to percolate on the Coleman stove. We left the kids in the tent and drove to the nearest Starbucks. But the first thing out of her mouth should not have been scorn, no matter how tempting. She should have said, after Art said he wanted to get dropped by a helicopter on a snowy mountain range: "Tell me more about that!" or, "Why is this important to you?" This would have furthered our discussion and ultimately brought us closer together. Instead, all further discussion was shut down by the dismissive remark.

Even though we may not agree with our spouse, we should be willing to hear his point of view, to listen attentively, and to try to understand. Fostering a *culture of appreciation* — which includes respecting the other person's thoughts and feelings and being open to accepting influence — builds strong relationships and happy marriages.

These communication techniques — the underlying positive, being empathic, and being open to influence — are really about making a commitment to keep communication alive. It's not so much a matter of technique, however, but rather a commitment to keeping the drawbridge down, to respecting ideas, feelings, and plans, and to furthering understanding so that love and intimacy can flourish. Keeping the drawbridge of communication down requires an investment in humility and some dying to ourselves.

## Forgiveness

Corrie ten Boom survived the horrors of Nazi concentration camps and was later able to forgive her captors personally. She describes in her memoir, *The Hiding Place*, a scene following the war in which one of her former captors, an SS guard who had mocked and abused her and her sister, came up to her after one of her talks and offered her his hand. She was filled with revulsion and didn't want to take it. "Jesus, I cannot forgive him," she prayed. "Give me your forgiveness." In that moment, she was able to shake his hand. And she writes, "And so I discovered that it is not on our forgiveness any more than on our goodness that the world's healing hinges, but on His. When He tells us to love our enemies, He gives, along with the command, the love itself." [5]

Most of us will never have to forgive someone for committing acts as atrocious as those of the Nazis during World War II. Yet in our marriages we have the opportunity to forgive — if not egregious crimes, then small affronts — many times over. "As many as seven times?" St. Peter offers, expansively. Jesus tells us, "I say to you, not seven times but seventy-seven times" (Matthew 18:21, NAB). And then he tells the parable of the servant who was forgiven his huge amount by his master but who refuses to have pity on his fellow servant, who owed him much less.

Forgiveness has one foot, as it were, in the natural arena and one in the supernatural. Many people have told Art in counselling that they cannot forgive their spouse for an egregious injustice: infidelity, pornography, abuse. The wounded spouse mistakenly thinks that he or she must experience a *feeling* of forgiveness. Yet forgiveness is, in one sense, a simple human action, a motion of the will: "I want to forgive you." Forgiveness does not require the absence of anger or an accompanying feeling of affection. The *feeling* of forgiveness may come later, or not at all. What is important is the will to forgive.

In his practice, Art has frequently counseled couples in which one partner has had an affair. Typically, the betrayed spouse is angry, devastated, and humiliated, though willing to at least try counseling in order to heal the marriage. These couples often have to face some disturbing truths about their marriage: one spouse looking down on the other, for example, or one idolizing the other, and both effectively preventing any *real* communication. In the best scenarios, the betrayer is deeply sorry, promises never to commit the sin again, and the couple learns (in therapy) how to communicate better. The wounded partner then finds the willingness to forgive — which does not, as Jesus showed us, entail endorsing the sin. "Then Jesus said, 'Neither do I condemn you. Go, [and] from now on do not sin any more'" (John 8:11, NAB).

Being willing to forgive over and over again is a foundation of marriage and the spiritual life, but asking for forgiveness is also essential. To do this effectively, it's necessary to sincerely express sorrow and actually *ask* for forgiveness, to repair the damage as best as able, and promise to make whatever changes are needed so the transgression does not happen again. Ultimately, genuine forgiveness depends on God's grace.

## Sacramental Grace

This brings us full circle, back to the early years of our marriage and our time in Germany. Being on the outskirts, foreigners in a country that didn't readily embrace either foreigners or children, we began (slowly, because we were rusty) to depend more and more on our faith and to read some of the great spiritual writers from a faith perspective rather than from an academic perspective.

Once we became active in our tight-knit Catholic community, we began to relish our faith even more. When we returned to the States, we were thrilled to feel once again comfortable and familiar with our surroundings, but we missed our small faith community. Now we were a drop in the bucket of a mega-parish with several thousand families. We knew from our European experience that — somehow — getting involved in our parish would help us feel more integrated and closer to our priests, our community. And being part of a faith community — being in communion with one another through our sharing in the Eucharist — actually (mysteriously) would bring us closer together as well, as it had in Germany.

We both found ourselves wanting to grow in our faith at the same time, and we attribute that to grace from the sacrament of marriage. Nonetheless, if you find yourself "unequally yoked," as St. Paul puts it (see 2 Corinthians 6:14), don't badger or heap derision on the spouse who is not yet where you are. This only serves to push him or her further away. Besides, there are likely some things about you that need work, too! In any case, we both reached the point that we were ready for a deeper step in our faith journey, but we didn't know exactly what. After meeting some inspiring homeschoolers, we decided to take on that challenge. Homeschooling itself was fraught with difficulties and isolating in many ways, both from the culture and from the neighborhood, yet it brought us to a community of vibrant Catholics who were practicing their faith in a lively and deeply committed way. We met happy families who inspired and challenged us.

It was another adventure, like the adventure that took us to Europe, only this time it was an adventure not in terms of physical place, but of the heart. We began seeking a personal relationship with Christ and, as Pope Francis writes, this is an occasion for joy: "The Lord does not disappoint those who take this risk; whenever we take a step toward Jesus, we come to realize that he is already there, waiting for us with open arms" (*Evangelii Gaudium*, 3).

We take the smallest step toward Christ, and He rewards us with an abundance of joy and laughter (and sufferings), friends and family, and adventures beyond our wildest imaginings. When we compare our rather self-centered, closed-in life before we fully embraced Christ and His Church with our life today (continually in need of conversion, of course), our present way is so much more joyful and rewarding. How could it not be, with Love at the center?

---

*Art Bennett is the president of Catholic Charities in the Diocese of Arlington, Virginia, and is a licensed marriage and family counselor with thirty years of experience in the mental health field. Laraine Bennett is a freelance writer and the author of* A Year of Grace: 365 Reflections for Caregivers. *The Bennetts have written numerous books together, including* The Temperament God Gave your Kids *and* The Temperament God Gave Your Spouse.

Chapter 3

# Stars in the Country Sky
## Contemporary Challenges to Marriage

By Brandon McGinley

Anthony was pretty psyched to have lost his virginity. At least that's what he wanted us to think.

Of my many college acquaintances, Anthony was one of the most liberated (as he would surely put it). And now he had put his "enlightened" view of sexuality into practice.

His excitement was evident, but it was clear when he announced his accomplishment to some of his much more traditional friends that he was subtly seeking our affirmation. It didn't take a licensed counselor to identify deep conflict lurking beneath the surface.

I was just beginning my reversion to the Catholic faith of my childhood at the time; this was one of several moments that demonstrated firsthand the real-life wisdom of the Church's teachings on sexuality. All the tensions in our sexual culture were on display: the assumed meaninglessness of sexual intimacy alongside the clear meaningfulness felt by Anthony; the perception of liberation alongside the reality of enslavement to cultural norms and seductive temptations; and the promise of fulfillment alongside the sensation of emptiness.

Anthony was a little hurt, though he shouldn't have been surprised, that we weren't able to give him the affirmation he was seeking. How could we? And anyway, the circumstances of this first sexual encounter taking place, as it did, within a fraught relationship were particularly damaging to him.

Now what does this story of college sexual confusion and liberation have to do with the contemporary challenges facing marriage?

## What Happens in Vegas

It's a tagline that has become a cultural touchstone: "What Happens in Vegas Stays in Vegas." The idea is simple enough: Las Vegas is more than a vacation from home — it's a vacation from your life. Whatever experiences you have there, you can shed them the moment you step onto the jetway at McCarran International Airport.

The concept is obviously fanciful, and yet our culture has taken it to heart. We apply it, explicitly or implicitly, everywhere. What happens in college stays in college. What happens during my bachelor years stays in my bachelor years.

A great deal of our entire sexual culture is built on this conceit — that we can compartmentalize our sexual experiences by geography, by maturity, or by whatever other artificial demarcation we dream up. This is how young people like Anthony permit themselves to do the celebrated "experimentation" we associate with college.

There's a scene in Terrence Malick's spellbinding *The Tree of Life* in which the neighborhood whippersnapper convinces the rest of the boys to strap a live frog to a bottle rocket. After it goes off, destroying the creature and somewhat discomforting the group, the troublemaker exclaims with triumph: "It was an experiment!" It's a clear attempt to evade responsibility for what they had done — in experimenting, all is permitted.

Like the boys in *The Tree of Life*, we want some parts of our lives — especially youthful sexual experimentation — not to count. We want to be able to dabble in this and dabble in that without consequences. What happens in Vegas stays in Vegas.

This is, however, not how things work. Our lives cannot be so easily divided up. The collection of memories and relationships and stories that build up over the course of our lives cannot, by our own will, be sawed off at convenient moments. Those things make up who we are as human beings.

Our culture tries to tell us that this is not so with regard to sexuality. Sex is harmless fun, they say, and it definitely won't have any lasting impact. But both science and lived experience demonstrate that precisely the opposite is true — sexual experiences form particularly lasting parts of who we are.

A friend told me about an acquaintance who pursued a very promiscuous lifestyle in her youth. Later in life this woman returned to the Catholic faith and married. She expected, as the culture teaches us, that she could leave behind all those previous experiences as if they were part of a past life. But they weren't; they were part of her life. And so, during intimacy with the husband she loved dearly she could not help but flash back to those many other men, like an involuntary slideshow.

This isn't just some kind of psychological abnormality. Chemicals are released during sexual encounters — in both men and women, though more so in women — that encourage feelings of trust and deep connection. Those chemicals, along with the intensity of sexual activity, create strong associations and memories that become part of us, whether we like it or not.

But to be honest, I don't think I need science to prove what lived experience already demonstrates. If sex were merely recreational and really not all that important, we'd have similarly vivid memories of our first tennis match as of our first sexual experience. I rest my case.

Those memories harm our ability later in life really to *be with* our spouse. He or she is one of many, inviting comparisons and unfair expectations no matter how hard we fight against them. I can't imagine what it would be like to look at my wife and see not her authentic self but only comparisons with all the other women with whom I had been intimate. If I had had such experiences, I know that's exactly what would have happened.

And we don't simply build up sexual experiences as we experiment; we also become accustomed to breaking off sexual relationships. We are told that a magical commitment switch will be flipped when the vows are read, and voilà, we'll be ready, for better or for worse. But if we've seen every relationship until now not as pointed toward marriage, but as aimless and contingent, then like it or not, that's how we will approach marriage. Living for others is not a gift bestowed on us by the wedding band; it is learned.

The tragedy in all of this is that people really want the stability, trust, and unconditional love that come with the Catholic vision of marriage. Nobody wants to see his or her spouse as the last of a series rather than just the one. Nobody wants to experience a marriage where both parties' sexual pasts are always present. Nobody wants to think divorce is always just around the corner. But under the spell of our culture's lies about sex and marriage we don't know how to avoid it. We think we can experiment; we think we can compartmentalize; we think we can get away with it. But we can't.

I hasten to recall that this chapter is about things that challenge our marriages, not things that doom them. Premarital promiscuity — often in the form of "serial monogamy," that is, several consecutive but exclusive sexual relationships — is not a death sentence for a healthy marriage. But it does put up substantial barriers to the type of marriage we all want.

If we want to overcome these challenges, there's no better place to start than with communication. This includes communication with our spouse, so that we can work through each other's difficulties together; communication with professionals, for those times when a counselor or therapist is needed to get to the root of the issues; and most of all communication with God, because through prayer we can lay all our struggles and suffering at His feet.

There is no silver bullet — only the hard and emotional work of building trust and understanding.

## A Bottomless Well

Even without the lingering effects of past sexual history, the challenges to marriage in contemporary society don't end after the exchange of rings and a big ballroom bash. No discussion of this topic would be complete without consideration of the omnipresent temptation of pornography.

I recently had lunch with two Catholic friends somewhat older than myself. The first, roughly middle-aged, recalled his atheist college days when *Screw* magazine arrived
at his door hidden in a brown paper cover. The second, a
little younger, pointed out that it wasn't piety that kept him
from pornography in his youth so much as the social em-
barrassment of driving to an "adult" bookstore, ducking
inside, selecting a product, and publicly emerging again. It
wasn't long ago that pornography, though available, was still
socially stigmatized.

But now as pornography has spread, our cultural barriers have fallen. In 2013 it was reported that 30 percent
of all Internet bandwidth was taken up with pornographic
content, and these sites attracted more visitors than Netflix,
Amazon, and Twitter combined. As more and more people
— according to Google, 70 percent of men and 30 percent
of women use Internet pornography — become accustomed
to porn, its social status has moved from the margins to the
mainstream. Porn companies know this and capitalize on
it: the infographic that contained these stats was produced
by a porn site under the title "Everyone You Know Watches
Porn."

The way we think about porn is best demonstrated
by a pop culture example. In one episode of the comedy *30
Rock*, the oddball variety show host Tracy Jordan thinks his
wife is pregnant with a daughter. This leads to a stunning
realization: all women are daughters. He resolves (unsuc-
cessfully, of course) to treat all women with more respect,
including no longer going to strip clubs. Beneath the humor
is the clear message that all people have dignity, and that
sexual objectification harms that dignity.

Meanwhile, throughout the program, pornography is
discussed nonchalantly — usually by the male characters,

married or single — as a normal aspect of everyday life. Never do any characters have the realization that Tracy has: that these women on the screen are real women. They are daughters, sisters, and even mothers.

We think that because the people on the screen are not physically present, pornography isn't *real* — really objectifying, really harmful, or really wrong. Nothing could be further from the truth.

Pornography is a bottomless well of empty promises. First, it promises that it will help, rather than impede, actual intimacy with your spouse. Then, it promises that it will fulfill your sexual needs that aren't currently being fulfilled. After that, it promises that it can be all that you want and need. And finally, it promises that with one more viewing of a slightly more perverse video, you will finally be satisfied.

Let's consider each of these promises.

Porn's first move is to suggest that it will get you in the mood and broaden your sexual horizons. But instead it short-circuits the intimacy and intimate communication that you ought to have with your spouse. It provides an easy route to sexual release in a fantasy world where your partner doesn't have feelings or vulnerabilities or the need to be loved. Porn presents an unrealistic view of sexuality that implants new desires that your spouse may not be willing or able to fulfill, cutting off the honest communication of preferences that leads to a mature and respectful relationship and (let's be honest) better sex.

Having seeded these new desires, porn then promises that it can fulfill them as a supplement to your spouse. But the fantasies of porn-land soon migrate from the laptop to the bedroom. Soon you are being physically intimate with your spouse, but mentally you're with your favorite performer. Soon your spouse becomes an inadequate stand-in for the naughty beauties of the screen.

This is when porn tells you it can be all you need. But we still value companionship, and so people often seek out those who can fulfill their pornographic desires. One woman told me about how her marriage ended after she discovered that her husband — a practicing Catholic and successful businessman — had hired a prostitute while on a business trip. She then discovered evidence of substantial use of Internet pornography. According to a spokesman for My House, a Catholic resource for overcoming pornography use, this is not an isolated example. "Sadly, I have talked to Catholic men whose pornography addiction led to infidelity and/or sexual contact with prostitutes."

Once porn has consumed you and deadened you to the actual people around you, it promises that the next, more stimulating experience will finally bring satisfaction. But as each slightly more depraved stimulation becomes commonplace, more is required. In her disturbing book *Pornified*, feminist journalist Pamela Paul ventures into the rabbit hole of online porn, describing in lurid detail the violence, the callousness, and the degeneracy of what is portrayed — and the men who can't get enough of it all. The well of empty promises is a black abyss.

But there is a ladder that leads back to daylight. The path the ladder takes is different for different people, but the first step is to realize you're tumbling into the abyss and to grab a rung. Don't worry; you won't be the only one.

Those who have kicked the porn habit recommend spiritual exercises, of course — prayer, Eucharistic adoration, the Sacrament of Confession. But they also recommend finding a group that can provide accountability, whether through your church or diocese or through a solid twelve-step program. Individualized professional counseling can also be very helpful and provide a setting for the honest communication with your spouse that is essential in overcoming the use of pornography. You are meant to help each other on your journey through this life and into the next; sexual struggles should (within reason) be an opportunity to practice that commitment, not an excuse to break it.

## But Nobody Told Me

How have we arrived at a moment when these challenges to marriage have become so acute for Catholics? It's actually pretty simple: both formal and informal catechesis — that is, the teaching of the truths of the Catholic faith — has been pitiful in regard to the nature and purpose of marriage and sexuality.

In their book *Marriage 911*, Greg and Julie Alexander describe how they found themselves on the brink of divorce. They had each been unfaithful and unhappy, and so separation seemed to be the natural next step. Conveniently at this critical moment, the visiting priest at their parish happened to be the diocesan official in charge of annulments. So, they scheduled a meeting.

They came away confused. Rather than immediately beginning the annulment proceedings, the priest gave them some homework: read up on what God's plan for marriage is and what the Church teaches about the sacrament of matrimony. They followed through by checking out the Bible, the *Catechism of the Catholic Church*, and other Church documents. What they found was a treasure trove of wisdom that pulled them through their darkest days and reignited their marriage. Inspired by their renewal, the Alexanders went on to found a ministry to help other married couples learn what the Church actually teaches about marriage.

But catechesis is about more than formal classrooms and ministries. The way we think about marriage is informed by the way those around us treat the institution. Remember my college friend Anthony? Like many, he was raised nominally Catholic and his parents had divorced some time before his arrival on campus. All he really knew was the failure of the Catholic vision of marriage — for him, such a vision was something between a bad joke and a wistful dream.

In a world where nearly half of marriages end in divorce, even among self-described Catholics, Anthony's story is a common one. Most Catholics have received neither formal instruction from the Church on the truth of marriage nor informal affirmation of the truth of marriage from their families, social circles, or the culture at large. This is the hidden challenge to marriage that precedes all others: most Catholics have little idea what marriage is or what it's meant to be.

This is where I'm supposed to inform you about the timeless wisdom of Church teaching on marriage in four hundred words or less. I could talk about how love is not just a feeling, but a chosen disposition toward your spouse that always says through word and action: "I want what's best for you." I could talk about how that authentic, self-giving love mirrors the unbroken love of the Father, Son, and Spirit in the ultimate community of the Trinity. I could talk about how in having children we can uniquely participate in God's perfectly self-giving love and creative power.

And all this would be true. I encourage you, whether or not you're experiencing struggles like the Alexanders, to follow their lead and to educate yourself on these and other issues pertaining to marriage. In addition to the *Catechism*, the beautiful papal document *Humanae Vitae* wouldn't be a bad place to start.

But what does all this really look like? What does it mean to be "self-giving"?

Here's a simple example: I'm a night owl, but my wife, Katie, is a morning person. At the end of the day I'm peppy, and she can be grumpy; at the beginning, she's peppy (*very* peppy), and I can be grumpy. But sometimes my strange sleep schedule catches up with me, and I pass out on the couch in the evening. Last time this happened, rather than waking me up to help with our infant daughter's bath and bedtime ritual (always a two-person job), she let me sleep.

It wasn't some kind of Hollywood moment of heroic self-sacrifice — but life isn't like that anyway. Real life is a collection of tiny actions that build up over time to form our character as well as the character of our relationships. In that everyday moment, Katie simply demonstrated that she's willing to go outside her comfort zone to do what's best for me — and not because this will place me in some kind of childish debt that I'll have to pay off by cleaning the bathroom, but because it was what I needed at that moment. That's self-giving love, authentic and unassuming.

The blogger Bonnie Engstrom tells another simple story: One night she was suffering from an overnight stomach bug that had her dashing to the bathroom. At one point she realized that her husband was no longer in bed; he was asleep on the floor in the hallway, barricading the door so none of their six children could climb into bed with their retching mommy. That's self-giving love, quiet and spontaneous.

The failure of catechesis can make the Catholic vision of marriage, especially the prohibition on artificial contraception, seem downright impossible. But it's precisely little devotions like these that prepare us for the greater sacrifices that will come our way. Love — whether of God, your spouse, or your neighbor — is more than something you feel; it's something you work at.

The work you put into the everyday aspects of marriage won't just help your relationship; it will demonstrate to an unbelieving culture that the Catholic vision of marriage is more than realistic: it's joyful and beautiful.

## With Great Challenges Come Great Opportunities

By this point, the state of marriage must seem pretty bleak. But it's precisely in this darkness — like gazing at the night sky out in the countryside — that the points of light shine brightest. Amid these challenges, those who pursue the Catholic vision of marriage stand out in deep contrast to the culture. In these difficult times, it is actually easier to be the signs of contradiction to worldly living that we are called to be.

We are the new counterculture: whether on a college campus or in the workplace, there is nothing more subversive than simply living out the Catholic vision of sexuality and marriage.

And the truth is that most people want the stability that comes with Catholic marriage, but they think it's no longer possible. By modeling joyful, faith-filled relationships, we show that authentic marriage is more than possible — it's wonderful. What we offer, even unconsciously, is evangelism-by-marriage: first people find Catholic relationships to be attractive, and then, with that cultural barrier having been overcome, they can consider the faith tradition that motivates and bolsters that appealing lifestyle.

This concept may seem obnoxiously optimistic, but I've seen it play out in real life. My friend Gregory represents all the beliefs we expect brilliant young people to hold: He's politically progressive, sexually "liberated," and spiritually agnostic. He's also uncommonly candid, which makes him a great case study.

For most of his college years, Gregory's disposition toward devout believers tracked with that of the culture: We're bigoted, out-of-touch with the world, and probably not terribly bright. Catholics were to him odd, almost mythical, creatures to be studied from afar. But then he joined a social club that just happened to include several faithful Catholics, and his caricatures were confronted with real people.

The fact of the matter is that Gregory, like nearly everybody, really wants someday to have a strong, loving, and committed marriage. He doesn't want to divorce, as his parents did. He doesn't want to have a distant, businesslike relationship with his wife. He desperately wants to be able to raise children in a stable and dynamic household. But he has no idea how to make all that happen. Our culture has a lot to say about liberation, but is quiet about the deep meaning and fulfillment that we all long for and that can best be found in joyful, self-sacrificing love.

And so these new Catholic friends were both challenging and appealing to him. They preached (over beers and burgers) and *lived*, to the best of their ability, ideas and lifestyles that took seriously the future they envisioned. They demonstrated a consistency within their philosophy, their day-to-day lives, and their long-term aims that Gregory's other friends and the culture at large lacked. And most of all they showed the authentic care for him as a person — that is to say, the love — that didn't seem to exist in the other superficial relationships in his life.

This Catholic community of single and married people in which Gregory has found himself, both in college and now in a new city, has presented him with an attractive and realistic alternative to the pleasurable but unfulfilling life the culture had been delivering to him. This has provoked a continuing crisis for him: Gregory's conscience has been awakened, but he can't yet let go of the hedonistic (I'm sure he would use this word, but nowadays with a touch of shame) lifestyle to which he has become accustomed.

The end of Gregory's story has yet to be written. But there is hope in large part because of the compelling witness of a Catholic community living purposefully in contradiction to our cultural consensus.

We all have Gregorys in our lives. It might be a Catholic sibling who has fallen away from the faith but is grasping in the dark for something to believe in. It might be a work colleague who says he just doesn't love his wife any longer. It might be an acquaintance with secret struggles who quietly looks to you and your marriage for guidance. It might even be your child's best friend whose parents are separated and who wants and needs to know that marriage can be joyful rather than spiteful.

As we work through the challenges to marriage that pervade our culture, it's helpful to remember that our efforts to make it work won't just impact ourselves and our families, but everyone around us. This should be a bracing realization, but a hopeful one.

The responsibility can seem overwhelming, but we must remember that we are not alone. "Fear not," God told Isaiah, "for I am with you" (41:10). With his aid, we cannot only overcome challenges to our own marriages, but we can reflect his light and love outward as a beacon of hope to a culture that desperately needs it.

---

*Brandon McGinley lives in Pittsburgh, Pennsylvania, where he works for the Pennsylvania Family Institute. He and his wife, Katie, welcomed their daughter, Teresa Benedicta, in July of 2013.*

Chapter 4

# Marrying Young
## From Central Park
## to the Confessional

By David and Amber Lapp

---

Amber:

A junior at a small Christian college in New York City, without a meal plan, David was skinny. But he was ten pounds lighter than he had been two weeks before — which put him at a scrawny 130 pounds. He was in love. And he couldn't eat. Sometimes he'd even throw up from butterflies and nervousness.

I had started to pick up on David's hints: the out of the blue phone call; the invitation to study together (on a Friday night of all nights); the long conversations we shared about theology.

So on a Sunday afternoon, after brunch with mutual friends, when David invited me to Central Park, I accepted.

It was a cold October day, deceptively so because the sun was shining brightly. I wore a short-sleeved black dress I had found in my grandma's closet, with only a cardigan and scarf for warmth, so I was grateful when David offered me his winter coat. ("He must like me!" I thought. His heart was pounding furiously, he recalls.)

On a wooden slat bench by Sailboat Pond, he made his intentions known. "Over the past few months of getting to know you...." He listed his favorite things about me, before asking, "Amber, would you give me the privilege of getting to know you better, of pursuing you?"

---

David and Amber:

Five months later we were in Iowa visiting Amber's family for Easter and talking about the future. At that point, we already knew we wanted to get married. And it made sense to us to get married after college graduation the following year — that way we could establish our post-grad life together. If we knew that we loved each other, trusted each other's characters, and shared similar views about the commitment of marriage, we didn't see much sense in waiting.

The hard part was convincing Amber's dad, who at the time acted like Steve Martin's character in *Father of the Bride*. David's $55,000 of student loans probably didn't make things any easier for him.

"Why don't you just enjoy your senior year, get a job, see where you end up, and then think about marriage?" he asked.

~

In the coming months, we struggled with feeling crazy for wanting to get married in our early twenties. In journal entries, Amber chronicled her fears that getting married early would mean being judged. "I want to get married right after college," she wrote. "But I don't think many people would respect such a decision.... I don't want to tell people that because I'm ashamed."

Amber had a strong desire to get married and to start a family relatively soon, but she worried that she might be selling herself short. After all, in the time period of 2005 to 2009, 80 percent of New York City twenty-somethings had never married.[6] But we also felt that if our grandparents had done it, David's parents had done it, and many others before us had done it, then we could do it, too.

David:

We spent the summer apart, Amber in Ohio and I in New York City. The distance solidified our intentions of marrying — and marrying young. After many more conversations, when I approached Amber's dad at the end of October 2008, he gave a hearty blessing — despite the fact that my Phillies were beating his Dodgers in the National League Championship Series.

So on October 28, 2008, a year after I had first declared my intentions, we found ourselves again in Central Park, seated at the wooden-slat bench by Sailboat Pond. It was rainy and cold and Amber had skipped a class for the anniversary date, which made her out of sorts. She wasn't expecting a ring on this rainy day.

But I began, "Amber, over the last year of getting to know you...." I echoed the words of our conversation the previous year, and for a moment Amber didn't catch on — until I knelt on one knee and pulled out a ring box.

"Amber, would you give me the privilege of sharing life with you?"

Half a year later, and three weeks after college graduation, we married. I was twenty-two, and Amber was twenty-one.

David and Amber:

"Dude, you married less than one year ago. I hope you don't feel obligated to stay married just beause [sic] of a public article," one commenter exclaimed in response to an essay David wrote for *The Wall Street Journal* — entitled "Did I Get Married Too Young?" — ten months into our marriage.

In the essay, David concluded:

> I may not have the freedom to globetrot at my own leisure or to carouse at a bar late into the night. But when I step into our five hundred-square-foot one-bedroom apartment, warmly lighted and smelling of fresh flowers and baked bread, I do have the freedom to kiss my beautiful wife and best friend — the woman I pledged to always love and cherish, and to raise a family with. I have no regrets.[7]

In response, we heard three main counterarguments.

1. Early marriage leads to divorce. The skeptic has a point: research shows that of women who got married below age twenty, 52 percent divorced. Of those who married between ages twenty to twenty-three, 34 percent divorced. By contrast, of those who got married at thirty and later, only 8 percent divorced.[8] *What about* that statistical reality?

2. You might be a different person at age thirty than you are at age twenty. If you marry young, you don't have time to really know yourself and to know what you want in a spouse.

3. Research shows that women especially could forfeit career success and financial independence by marrying young.[9]

These objections remind us of our friend Derek. Derek remembers his wife, Leslie, asking a few years into their marriage, "Did we get married too young?" They had married when he was twenty-three, she was twenty.

"I want to be young," said Leslie, who frequently went out drinking for the night with her single friends. She talked about how she wanted to travel with her friends — all of whom were single — and about how she was still finding herself. She told Derek that she wasn't really sure who she was as an individual, so how could she figure that out as a married person?

"You're just saying what the culture does," he remembers saying. "That's not the same thing as what you're supposed to do."

Soon, Leslie was hanging out with another man. Derek grew suspicious, and one day asked Leslie, "Who would you say that you have more romantic feelings for — me or John?"

"John," she responded.

Derek was devastated, but wanted to make their marriage work. After months of trying to save their marriage, however, they divorced.

Stories like Derek and Leslie's make us wonder: is it folly to marry young in a culture that puts a premium on "finding yourself" during your twenties?

Derek thinks it all depends on one's "presuppositions" about marriage. In other words, *how you think* about marriage is even more important than *when* you get married. Derek thinks that if someone believes we're just "free agents floating through," and sometimes love lasts and sometimes it doesn't, and "it really just depends on how you're feeling" — then getting married is "stupid." But, he continues, if two people believe that marriage "should last until you're dead" — then marriage makes sense.

The idea that what matters most is not marriage age but marriage *beliefs* struck us in our conversations with seniors, many of whom married in their late teens or early twenties and struggled financially and went on to celebrate their golden anniversaries. As our eighty-year-old neighbor, Lois, said with fire in her eyes and a wag of her finger, "Well, I tell you what, when I got married, it was for better or worse, for richer or poorer, in sickness and in health, until death do us part. That's what was on my mind — till death do you part!"

*It all depends on one's presuppositions.*

⁓

It's an important point, because behind most objections to early marriage is a particular understanding of what marriage is, and of how the human person "finds himself."

In contemporary American culture, the dominant view of marriage is the consumer view. Bill Doherty, a marriage therapist at the University of Minnesota, notes how the market model of life now invades almost every area of life — including marriage.[10] In the consumer view, the marriage is valuable only so long as one's needs are being met. Thus, Doherty observes how we have moved from being "citizens" of marriage to consumers of marriage. In other words, we've gone from asking, "What can I do for my spouse?" to, "What can my spouse do for me?" The problem, as Doherty points out, is that consumers are inherently disloyal. In a world of many options, it's difficult to resist the alluring logic of consumerism, which invites us to think, "My needs aren't being met. I deserve better."

It's an easy trap to fall into. About a year and a half into our marriage, we were walking on the fairgrounds, watching teenage girls carrying bears won by their boyfriends at the clown toss, couples nestled in the Ferris wheel, and even a few making out behind the vendors' stands.

"Remember when we were that in love?" David asked.

*Were?* The comment bothered Amber. Later, when a neighbor, muscular and tattooed, started flirting with her, she felt butterflies for him, and resentment toward David. She felt like David wasn't meeting her emotional needs. We talked and fought through it until we came to an understanding and a promise to not take each other for granted — but the question had flashed through her mind: "What would it be like to be with the neighbor?"

However, in his book *The Paradox of Choice: Why More Is Less*, psychologist Barry Schwartz sheds some light on why the consumer's quest for more and better options does not necessarily equal more happiness.[11] Bewildered by an array of choices, we find ourselves constantly wondering, *"What if?"* We have buyer's remorse. While choice is supposed to liberate us, too many choices can actually tyrannize us. This is what Schwartz calls the "paradox of choice."

By committing to each other, a married couple limits their choices — but in doing so submit to a truer logic: the paradox of gift. The paradox of gift says that in *giving* the ultimate gift (ourselves), we *gain* what humans throughout the centuries have seen as one of the most precious gifts of life — the love of one's spouse and children. When it would seem that we lose ourselves, we find ourselves.

Which brings us to the Catholic vision of marriage. In the Catholic view, marriage is a radically generous union that joins spouses in body and soul, and that includes openness to children. The Catholic tradition proposes that marriage is not a ticket to one's own version of self-fulfillment, but an invitation to holiness. What if your future wife becomes paralyzed? What if your child gets cancer? Marriage makes heroes, not consumers.

The Catholic vision is thus more rigorous — and rewarding — than the consumer view. While the latter is like shopping for select produce at the grocery store, the former is like a plot of land that invites a couple to pick up their spades, get their hands dirty — and after much patience and perseverance — to enjoy the fruit of their labor. Instead of merely consuming the produce, the Catholic vision of marriage invites one to husband his plot of land, to practice husbandry. As Wendell Berry notes, in its original use, to husband means "to use with care, to keep, to save, to make last, to conserve."[12]

The Catholic vision invites a couple to care for and to keep their union, to save and to make last, to conserve until death does them part. This requires the discipline and patience of a good farmer. But it also brings with it the joys of fruitfulness.

---

David:

The flameless vanilla candles from Walgreens shimmered in the darkness. Bach played on the iPod as I massaged Amber. We felt like we were in a sanctuary, a temple, a very holy place. Just as Jewish tradition says that God's Spirit hovers over the marriage bed, so we felt something like God's presence hover over the labor bed. The comparison is apt: the midwife Ina May Gaskin describes childbirth as a kind of ecstasy[13] — the ecstatic completion of the ecstatic act that created the child in the first place.

But Amber's condition was critical. She had HELLP syndrome, and her liver enzyme levels were rising, risking liver rupture.

After twenty-four hours of labor, Amber was still only seven centimeters dilated. The doctor — tall and thin and looking like he was straight out of "Grey's Anatomy" — pursed his lips and said, "We might have to section you. But … I'll give you another hour."

That next hour was Amber's heroic moment. She felt a burst of energy and spoke and sung to her baby, Daniel, telling him that it was all right, he could come out now. He started kicking and moving. Amber felt an intense pressure and stretching. "He's coming down!" she said. "Where is the doctor?"

Two hours of pushing later, Daniel's head emerged. But he was stuck; he had shoulder dystocia, another obstetrical emergency. "I've got this!" our midwife yelled, and she reached inside, repositioned Daniel, and pulled his white, waxy body out safely.

Then there was another emergency. "Call the doctors back in," our midwife ordered. Amber was hemorrhaging blood. In a frenzied flurry, two people pushed on her stomach like they were kneading dough vigorously; but all we could do was stare at the baby in the warmer.

"My baby! My baby! We have a baby!" Amber cried, and then laughed, and then did some combination of the two as I kissed her and joined in the laughter. Neither of us noticed the hemorrhaging, so great was our joy. We literally found ourselves united in the reflection we saw in our child. Our love now lived and breathed in Daniel. As Karol Wojtyla (now St. John Paul II) said, "The lover 'goes outside' the self to find a fuller existence in another."[14]

Marriage calls a man and woman to give the gift of "I" — a gift so radical that it constrains our choice, but also so creative that it creates a "we" (the one-flesh marriage union) and other little "I's" (children). The decision of marriage at once narrows the horizons (you can't marry anyone else) and extraordinarily expands them (you create a new family). Marriage is a paradox of gift.

It is also a call to holiness.

"I baptize you in the name of the Father, and of the Son, and of the Holy Spirit," the priest intoned as he poured the sacred water over Daniel's head two months after his birth. "You have become a new creation, and have clothed yourself in Christ."

---

David and Amber:

"Honey, how can you expect me to watch Danny, work twenty hours a week, grocery shop, cook, pay our bills, *and* wash the dishes? Can't you at least keep the kitchen clean?" Amber groans, her voice rising with the pronouncement of each task, as David lounges in the living room, reading *The End of Men: And the Rise of Women*. He can't believe the incompetency of these guys Hanna Rosin interviewed!

"Honey, how many times do I have to tell you, use the same cup for each day!" bellows David from the kitchen, while Amber is in the office trying to finish a chapter for our book about the relationship and family struggles of young adults. "The dishwasher shouldn't be this full!"

"Bless me, Father, for I have sinned," we ask in the confessional, trusting in Jesus' faithfulness. Forgive me, we say to each other, as we lay in bed, toes touching, helping us find our way back to each other.

---

Amber

When we enter church, Danny likes to dip his fingers into the small baptismal font, and as he attempts the sign of the cross — a touch on his forehead, and a vigorous, repeated rubbing of his chest — we smile with joy, and recall our own baptism.

"You have become a new creation, and have clothed yourself in Christ."

---

David and Amber:

"Honey, we're always late!" David steams in fury, as Amber dries her hair. It's 8:56, Mass starts at 9:00, and it's a fifteen minute drive.

"David, you always wait until the last minute to get ready!" Amber shrieks, as they finally burst out the door at 11:00 a.m. for the ten-hour drive to Gatlinburg, three hours after we intended to leave. As we drive off for the week-long vacation, shouting at each other, David notices that the front door is still open, and Amber rolls her eyes in wrath.

"Bless me, Father, for I have sinned," we ask again in the confessional, accepting Jesus' mercy and each other's.

Back and forth it goes: "You have become a new creation...." "Bless me, Father, for I have sinned." Baptism and penance, sin and salvation — the rhythm of our married lives.

At the time of this writing, David is twenty-six, Amber twenty-five. Our marriage is not all flowers and fresh-baked bread. It is a field of love, where we are cultivating the very love that David first declared and Amber reciprocated on that fall day in Central Park — through a hundred ordinary gestures of charity over thousands of days that become a lifetime of years. Our marriage is the place where, as the *Catechism of the Catholic Church* says, "one learns endurance and the joy of work, fraternal love, generous — even repeated — forgiveness, and above all divine worship in prayer and the offering of one's life" (1657).

But how does any of this answer the objections to early marriage?

If you think about marriage as a consumer — like picking select produce that will give the most savory satisfaction — then marrying in your early to mid-twenties might just increase chances for divorce. And if you think of the path to finding yourself as a solitary search for self, you may find marriage stifling. But if you go "back to the land," if you switch from consumer to cultivator — if you think of marriage as a good farmer — then everything changes. Because that person, no matter what age he gets married, is like a devoted localist: he finds and wins his beloved place on this earth, he prepares the soil well, and upon *that* plot of land he takes his stand, he pours forth all his love and care, for better or worse, in abundance and famine, 'til death does him part.

The good farmer does not exploit the land for his own profit, but enters into a relationship with the land, respecting and helping its organic cycles of growth: sowing time and harvest time, barrenness and fruitfulness. So the good spouse does not use his beloved for his own emotional and sexual satisfactions, but enters into a genuine relationship with the beloved, respecting and helping his organic growth in holiness: baptism and penance, sin and salvation.

Think of marriage like a good farmer, and early marriage becomes less daunting. Because there are habits we can cultivate that, statistically, predict success in marriage. For instance, in one study, a couple's robust attitudes about commitment emerged as the best predictor that a couple was not prone to separation or divorce.[15]

Another study found that couples who wait until marriage to have sex report better communication, sex, relationship satisfaction, and relationship stability than their peers who had premarital sex.[16] Further, couples who say that "God is at the center of our marriage" are more likely to be very happy in their marriages and less likely to be divorce-prone.[17]

But what about the third objection — that early marriage might demand career sacrifices? There is no one-size-fits-all answer to this objection. For us, getting married and establishing our "family path" was more important than establishing independent career paths. We agreed that we would go to the city where one of us found a better job. If that meant David turning down a job elsewhere because Amber found a better job in New York City, David was willing to work at Starbucks if necessary. And the same was true for Amber.

As it happened, we each found jobs in New York City after college graduation and, about a year into marriage, we were working together on a research project about marriage at a New York think tank. While we knew the opposite might happen, for us, getting married turned out to help our career path. And with our common purse and shared motivation, marriage spurred us to pay off $55,000 of student loans in two years.

But some people may discern a calling to a career that makes great demands on their time and resources, and they may judge it imprudent to get married in their early- to mid-twenties. After all, there is no rule that all those called to marriage must get married by, say, twenty-five. There are good reasons for waiting to get married until one's late twenties, or afterward — for instance, pursuing work that is incompatible with early marriage, waiting for a suitable mate, discerning if you are called to the vocation of marriage. For these people, it's true that early marriage may not be a wise idea. But people who take this path are also called to chastity, and are called to offer their single years in service to others — not as a license to serve selfish desires.

But if you find yourself in love, and you want to love, let yourself be taken by your beloved, win your beloved, discern character, and seek the counsel of the wise in your life. Don't delay marriage just because you think getting married in your early- to mid-twenties is too early, or because you find yourself thinking (like a consumer), "I want to keep my options open." Embrace heroic husbandry.

Families and communities must also embrace and support couples who marry early. Because while marriage beliefs are important, those beliefs aren't formed and maintained in a vacuum. They develop in families and communities. For instance, we are indebted to our parents and grandparents for modeling good marriages. And when we left them, we set off for a college community where we enjoyed strong friendships that challenged us to lives of holiness. Then, after we got married, we lived within a ten-minute walk of four other young married couples whom we respected.

It is imperative, especially in today's divorce culture, that young couples be surrounded by such "friends of marriage."[18] Given our generation's fears of commitment, of divorce, of children even, friends of marriage can remind young couples that marriage is not about achieving perfect happiness, but about striving together toward holiness. And with such a perspective, early marriage is nothing to be afraid of.

One night shortly after Danny's birth, Amber was afraid for her health, afraid to have more children, and unable to sleep. So she asked David to read to her. He flipped open the nearest book, a collection of sayings from St. Josemaría Escrivá, and happened to open to this: "You share in the creative power of God: that is why human love is holy, good and noble…. Each child that God grants you is a wonderful blessing from Him: don't be afraid of children!"[19]

Don't be afraid of love. Don't be afraid of marriage. Don't be afraid of children. We share in the creative power of God.

That's why four years into early marriage — with Danny dancing on the bed, and another miracle somersaulting in Amber's womb — dude, we have no regrets.

---

*David and Amber Lapp are Research Fellows at the Institute for Family Studies and Affiliate Scholars at the Institute for American Values. They blog at Family-Studies.org and IBelieveinLove.com. Their work has appeared in media outlets such as* The Wall Street Journal, Huffington Post, National Review, *and* First Things.

# Chapter 5

# *Are You Done?*
## *Catholic Marriage and Contraception*

By Jenny Uebbing

~

"Are you done?" she asked.

I looked askance at the well-meaning lady in the Target checkout line beaming an over-caffeinated morning smile in my direction.

*Am I done?* I wondered, looking down at the pile of crap winging its way down the conveyor belt to the accompanying tune of dollar signs being sucked out of my bank account. I shrugged and wondered if she was being philosophical. Is one ever truly "done" shopping at Target, after all? Is one ever fully done becoming the person she was created to be? Works in progress, those.

Suddenly I realized she must be talking offspring. Specifically, the two precariously balanced blondies in the cart and my burgeoning belly. *Ohhhh. Am I done? Thaaaat's what she's wondering.*

"Heh, we'll see." Was the best I could muster. Other encounters have yielded more or less confrontational answers, such as, "God only knows," or, "I sure hope not, they're kind of fun." And once, when I was feeling particularly socially engaging: "Nah, we're just getting warmed up!"

I generally tend toward the vague less-is-more answer with strangers, however, realizing that they're just trying to make conversation and probably feeling the need to comment on my amazing and obvious ability to produce children. I try not to dwell on the reality that we're basically discussing my sex life, these strangers and I, and that what they're really wondering is whether and what kind of birth control I'm using, and if I realize it isn't very "effective." And who knows, maybe they're just hoping to run into the next Duggar family.

This encounter could have been any of the dozens of similar encounters I've had since birthing baby number two last year and, frankly, what used to incense me in theory hardly even elevates my blood pressure in practice these days.

If only these well-intentioned (or even malevolently intentioned) observers could see into my heart, and into the depths of my selfishness and struggle, they'd know without a doubt that I am nowhere close to being "done." Not with mothering, and not with slowly, painfully, incrementally growing in patience and experience and — please God — holiness, in the gritty pancake-batter-encrusted day-in-and-day-out of it all.

I wonder if anybody realizes what a weird thing this is to ask someone whether or not they're "done" having children. I guess if motherhood and marriage were recognized more widely as vocations rather than current occupations, it wouldn't be such a common mistake. Imagine how weird it would be to ask your pastor after Mass one Sunday if he were "done" preaching homilies. Or asking a couple celebrating their thirtieth wedding anniversary whether they were "done" being married.

Motherhood, at a fundamental level, is not just something you do; it's something that you are. And just as priests preach and confer the sacraments and married couples live their vows and pick each other's wet towels up off the end of the bed, mothers have — and mother — children.

God, in His Divine generosity and possibly, Lord forgive me, foolishness, has seen fit to give me three beautiful babies to mother so far. Who am I to assume that He won't give me more, or even worse, to presume that He *will* eventually, and try to manipulate my present circumstances in such a way as to frustrate His will?

I guess part of what always surprises me is the assumption that everyone seems to be making that sex and babies are something that are only very occasionally paired together, and that one can't be too careful in planning for said offspring. Color me reckless, but I'm not buying it.

## Tough to Swallow

Growing up Catholic, I had a pretty clear idea of the Church's teaching on love, sex, and babies, thanks to my parents who lived it clearly for my six siblings and me to see. I was something of an anomaly at the large public university I attended simply because I was *not* on the Pill, while most of my friends definitely were.

One evening while I was in college, I was out making a quick grocery run when I looked down at my phone to see a text from my roommate: "Can u grab my prescription? I'm almost out."

My heart sank, because I knew she was asking me to pick up her next pack of birth control pills, and I wondered how I could possibly get out of it. Making up some lame excuse about needing proof of ID for the pharmacist, I escaped the store without her Ortho, but felt a heaviness on my heart. I was under no illusion that she and I were on the same page morally, but that didn't alter my intuition that this stuff — this magic pill that was supposed to set her free — was actually the source of many of the woes plaguing her personal life.

I'd come to suspect that there was more to the Church's teaching on contraception than a simple "thou shalt not." I was beginning to realize that women I knew — my friends and their sisters and some of my own family members — were being harmed by this supposedly miraculous "formula for freedom."

This stuff we're being sold as a means to free us from the slavery of childbearing is actually shackling us to a different tyrant: the illusion of control. Every time a woman pops that daily pill (or rolls up her sleeve for that yearly implant) she does so under the impression that she is the one calling the shots. Her body, her choice, her timing … and her risk. To her health, to her relationships, and ultimately, to the one relationship that matters most.

Everyone knows the Pill and other forms of hormonal contraception carry myriad risks and dangers. Even the secular press is beginning to acknowledge this. In January 2014, for example, *Vanity Fair* carried a devastating article by a grieving mother whose twenty-four-year-old daughter died of pulmonary embolisms, "one of thousands of suspected victims of the birth control device NuvaRing." But few people know, or care to admit, the emotional and spiritual dangers associated with contraception.

## Is It Safe?

I had the good fortune to deliver my second born, John Paul Francis, in a Catholic hospital staffed by some of the very best nurses in the world. We had a few minor complications after his birth, and the staff was unbelievably loving and impeccably professional. With one exception. Early in the afternoon on the first day of JP's ex-utero life, a brisk knock startled us from our breastfeeding reverie. I looked up to see an efficient looking woman with a clipboard letting herself into our recovery room; and while I struggled to cover up, she began flipping through the pages of my chart, rattling off routine post-natal questions.

"What kind of birth control will you be using?"

Her question startled me, sandwiched in between inquiries into the health of the pregnancy and previous breastfeeding successes or struggles.

"Excuse me?"

"What will you be using for protection?" she prompted again, pen poised to record my response.

I think I actually laughed at her, so ridiculous did the situation appear in my drugged, exhausted, and post-euphoric state.

"Um, we don't use contraception. And sex is pretty much the last thing on my mind right now."

She flashed me a tight-lipped smile and let the matter drop, but we would be asked *five* more times before our discharge about our plans for birth control. Finally, fed up, Dave summoned a hospital official to our room and explained patiently that we were practicing Catholics, that we were very much aware of the "risks" and "dangers" of conception, as evidenced by our mewling three-day-old son, and could somebody *please* make a note in my chart to stop asking us this silly question.

Lying there in my hospital bed, swollen and emotional and clutching my new baby, I don't think I've ever been more attracted to my husband, or more grateful for his love for me. *All* of me. Dangerous baby-making parts and all. I wished I could explain that to the hospital officials who were so eager to sterilize that love that flows between us. The same love that had produced the plump, swaddled bundle resting in my arms. For a place dedicated to the delivery and care of new life, their maternity unit seemed pretty freaked out by the idea of married couples having sex.

Here's the thing though; God didn't intend that each and every sexual act result in a new car seat in the back of your mini-van. That's just not the way it was designed. Sex does not always guarantee pregnancy, contrary to what Planned Parenthood — along with some well-meaning medical professionals — want us to believe. Women, unlike men, aren't fertile 365 days a year. Natural Family Planning, or NFP, a scientifically developed method for monitoring a couple's fertility, can help a couple choose to postpone or achieve pregnancy via simple observations of naturally occurring signs in a woman's cycle. A tad more civilized than popping a pill or surgically shutting down a bodily system, at least from a medical perspective.

## Raise Her Right

I have some of my most interesting conversations in retail establishments. Nothing says "chat me up" quite like taking your kids out in public, and on this particular morning in Grease Monkey, the waiting room's sole other occupant, a friendly gentleman, struck up a conversation.

"Is he the only one?" he asked, pointing toward my oldest.

I awkwardly put my hand over my still flat midsection and smiled, admitting that another baby was going to be joining our party.

"Another boy?" prompted my new friend.

"Uh, well, it's too soon to tell, heh heh, we'll see."

"Hope it's a boy … girls are crazy. Impossible with a girl!"

I nodded emphatically, not because I agreed with him that all females were, indeed, very crazy, but because I myself was once a teenager from hell and, judging from his age and appearance, I had a hunch he was currently in the trenches with a high-school-aged daughter.

"My daughter, she wants to go to the parties, wear the skinny jeans that come down and show her belly, everything … she tells me all the time 'I hate you,' 'Why can't I do what my friends are doing?' 'What are you doing in my room?' I tell her I'm her father; it's *my* room … I'm just lending it to you."

He sat back, looking satisfied, before continuing.

"Last week I told her, ask me again on Saturday night about a rave … and I'll give you a reason why you can't go."

He went on to explain that she had come to him again that past Saturday evening, begging to be allowed to go out with her friends. Telling her to grab her jacket, he led her to his truck and ferried her out to the abandoned warehouse district where he knew the festivities were being held. As they pulled up they could hear techno music spilling out into the night, and drunk party-goers were stumbling all over the dark parking lot.

Turning to his daughter, the father asked her what she saw, and she was silent.

"You see those men?" he asked her. "Those are men thirty, thirty-five years old. They've been drinking. I don't know who they are. Do you know what happens to you if I let you go to someplace like this? You get raped. Or worse.

And even if I come and find you, it might be too late. Is that what you want?"

He looked pained as he recounted the story, and I have to admit to being simultaneously impressed with his parenting technique and terrified of eventually parenting a daughter, God-willing.

I told him she was lucky, that more girls needed to have dads looking out for them, and he nodded solemnly.

And then he said the weirdest thing.

Leaning forward, he confided, "I don't want to raise, you know, *virgins* or something, but I want her to be happy, to wait … to find a really good guy, not just get pregnant. I tell her 'you come to me when you are ready, I'll get you the Pill, whatever.'"

Dumbfounded, I collected my thoughts while he got up to pay at the counter. He turned and continued talking to me as the cashier rang him up.

Clearing my throat, I volunteered the information that, you know, those hormonal pills are really bad for young girls' bodies, to which he nodded in agreement.

We barely had time for another couple sentences before he was out the door, but as he left he told me good luck with my little guy, and I told him to keep his little girl safe … and I scratched my head in disbelief.

Here was this perfect stranger, pouring his heart out to me about holding his children to a higher standard than the culture around them and protecting them from harm, and then he admitted to being willing to enable her physical, psychological, and moral decline "when she was ready."

How did we get here? How was this man — by all appearances a real man in a sea of little boys just playing at parental authority — willing to equip his young daughter with the very means by which she could destroy her life?

How deeply ingrained the contraceptive mentality has become in our culture. Thirty years ago no father in his right mind would have discussed — with a stranger in an auto-care lobby — enabling his adolescent daughter's sexual activity.

We have swallowed a monstrous lie in the form of a little Pill. And even while bemoaning the general state of moral decline in our society, we quietly condone it by handing our children the necessary equipment to screw up their lives and hearts, often losing them in the process.

And yet this is what most parents believe will keep their kids safe. Not chastity, not virtue, not common sense and a little old fashioned self-control, but a Pill to prevent pregnancy. As if *that's* the worst thing that can happen to a sexually active fourteen-year-old.

The crazy thing is, what this dad perceived as a means to keep his little girl safe, many married couples wield in the bedroom to protect themselves from one another. Which leads me to wonder when, in our culture, is sex ever considered truly "safe?"

## What Happiness Is Made Of

My husband and my kids are not only the people closest to me — they're my vocation, in a very real sense. I look at them and see God's wager that with their help and His grace, I might actually have a shot at eternal happiness, and at happiness in this life — the real kind, not the glossy-magazine kind.

I don't feel the need to protect myself from them. I love them desperately, and even when it is painful, I desire their happiness above my own. More often than not, in so doing, I end up far happier than when I act selfishly — even when it's inconvenient. *Especially* when it's inconvenient.

This past summer we had the opportunity to take the vacation of a lifetime. We were living in Rome, Italy, at the time, and I received an unexpected e-mail from an old acquaintance. She and her new husband would be honeymooning on the Amalfi Coast in July, and asked if we wanted to house swap with them for four days while they explored Rome from our apartment near the Vatican? Um, yes please. Giddy at the thought of a stretch of uninterrupted beach days in one of the world's most beautiful stretches of coastline, we optimistically over-packed one heavy suitcase and made haste to the train station, toddlers in tow.

The first night of our romantic getaway, the two-year-old spiked a 102-degree fever. We got very little sleep, and our quaint cliff-side villa with the expansive terrace overlooking the sparkling Mediterranean felt more like a prison cell by 3:00 a.m. The morning found us bleary-eyed but beach hungry, and as we loaded Tylenol into our son's system, we packed our beach bag for the winding descent into the town center and the waiting beach. I think we lasted all of forty-five minutes that first morning, slathering repeated applications of sunscreen on both boys and watching with bated breath as the fussy one-year-old took a downhill turn, following his older brother into virus land.

Defeated, we trudged back up the cliff side with our sopping towels, now with a matching pair of miserable, glassy-eyed toddlers.

I think we clocked in around four hours of sleep that night, punctuated by a fruitless late-night run to the town's sole *farmacia* only to find it very much closed for the evening. By afternoon of day three we were barely coherent, looking at each other over the feverish blonde heads of sleeping babies sprawled in various corners of the apartment. This was the least romantic getaway I could have fathomed. The gentle Mediterranean breeze fluttering the curtains over the balcony seemed to mock our misery, taunting us with fantasies of child-free beach combing and sun bathing on the umbrella-dotted expanses lining the coast in both directions.

But the kids were asleep. Finally. Dave raised a hopeful eyebrow in my direction and motioned toward the small, empty bedroom in the back of the apartment. *You've got to be kidding me*, I thought to myself. That was the very *last* thing on my mind after the past seventy-two hours of hell we'd been through. And yet … it *was* vacation. And they were sleeping.

Later that afternoon, when the patients had arisen from their feverish slumbers, we headed down to the town piazza for dinner. The kids were still fairly miserable, but their fevers had broken. And as Dave and I held hands and watched them toddle around on the cobblestones, I felt a sense of satisfaction deeper than anything I recalled from our idyllic Hawaiian honeymoon. This was our life now, and it was still romantic, perhaps even more so, albeit in a consolatory kind of way. I rested my weary head on his shoulder and watched our boys play, happy that I'd said yes earlier that afternoon, and feeling closer to him and more peaceful than I had in weeks.

We were in this together, for the long haul. And sometimes real love means squinting in the darkness to read dosing recommendations on infant Motrin, and sneaking in opportunities for romance when they present themselves, however unassumingly.

## How's That Working Out for You?

There's no denying contraception is here to stay. But it's time we took a look around and performed a cultural self-evaluation of what it has delivered in the past fifty years or so of widespread acceptance and availability.

Are our marriages healthier? Are our families thriving? Are couples more attached to one another, more sexually satisfied, and more likely to stick it out for the long haul in this crazy adventure called Holy Matrimony?

I think the numbers speak for themselves. Since the Pill came on the market, the rate of divorce has risen, more or less steadily, and in direct correlation.

There may be more people having sex, thanks to the Pill, but the overall quality seems to have suffered rather dramatically. Divorce is rampant, pornography is pandemic, and abortion is becoming more commonly accepted as a "viable option" when things don't go as planned. In short, we're in sexual free-fall, and there seems no immediate end in sight.

There has to be a better way to go about this whole marriage business.

I believe it is the Catholic Church's understanding that children are good, that marriage is good, and that the two are intertwined to such an extent that separation is neither advisable nor feasible without damaging both.

A radical message? Perhaps. But it's a message that the world is hungry to hear. Glutted on sex that is supposedly free from consequences, never have so many people been so starved for real love and lasting happiness.

Maybe the best place to begin the conversation, whether with your spouse, your sister, or your coworker, is in terms of happiness, a common currency if ever there was one. Ask them — and ask yourself — are you happy? Does living this way truly fulfill you? Or do you imagine there could be a better way to go about this love and sex business?

And then be prepared for some really interesting conversations. Because if there's one thing bringing up contraception is sure to accomplish, it's further discussion. And it's a conversation that's worth having, that's long overdue, and that could bear surprising fruit. Maybe even fruit that needs a name, nine months down the road.

---

*Jenny Uebbing is the content editor for Heroic Media News and a columnist for Catholic News Agency and Catholic Exchange. She and her husband David reside in Denver with their young family, where she blogs at* Mama Needs Coffee *and reheats the same shot of espresso three times a day.*

Chapter 6

# *Getting to Know You*
## *Convenience, Commitment, and Cohabitation*

By Meg T. McDonnell

"I'm really glad I decided not to live with him," my friend (I'll call her Madison) said to me as she fiddled with the plastic lid of her half-empty take-away coffee cup.

We had just finished talking about a disagreement that had taken place between her and her then-boyfriend. The disagreement wasn't a make it or break it moment for the relationship, but it had opened her eyes to some communication issues the two of them needed to work through — issues related to individual growth as well growth as a couple. By having their own apartments to retreat to, Madison and her boyfriend had the time and space to allow such individual growth to occur.

I could tell she was relieved to have her own place, but her statement about the possibility of living together surprised me. Madison and her boyfriend were raised in Catholic families and both still attended Mass every Sunday. Both of them had attended Catholic schools for at least part of their education. Both sought to build a relationship with God and to integrate Him into their daily lives. She knew that sex before marriage was against Church teaching and, by association, so was living together.

But, in her case, their practical situation tempted them to justify it. He needed a new roommate and they intended to get married soon, so the thought of saving money and the time spent traveling to each other's apartments was tempting.

Cohabitation is a new normal in the twenty-some-things' dating script, and it's so pervasive in the culture that even "in the pew" Catholics are "trying it on" before marriage. According to the Center for Disease Control (the federal government's record keeping agency that includes data on living arrangements and marriage), 57 percent of never-married women and 60 percent of never-married men cohabited prior to their first marriage.[20]

Being a twenty-something myself, I have many family members and friends who have lived with their romantic partners prior to marriage, and I doubt I have a peer who can't say the same. My parents have even remarked to me that they'll sometimes ask new friends or colleagues if their kids are married and will get the response "living together" in a tone that indicates a close similarity to marriage.

But as the old saying goes, "Just because everyone is doing it, doesn't mean it's right." Yet sometimes, individuals don't always know why it's wrong. In the case of my friend Madison and her boyfriend, even though they'd already decided against living together, our conversation over coffee was perhaps the first time she came to see concretely *why* living together before marriage wasn't a good idea.

## We vs. Me

When a man and a woman decide to marry, they are committing to a life that is no longer just for oneself, but also for another. They think no longer for "I" but for "we." Cohabitation imitates the actions of marriage, but without the promise of forever and the full commitment of that "we."

"No one can simulate self-giving," says marriage and family expert Dr. Jennifer Roback Morse. "Half a commitment is no commitment. Cohabiting couples have one foot out the door, throughout the relationship."

But for many young individuals, this "half commitment" isn't always apparent at first. And it can be devastatingly heartbreaking when it shows its face in the relationship — whether that be in the dating stage or in marriage.

Take my friends' (I'll call them Liz and Drew) experience with cohabitation. They had been dating for several months leading up to college graduation. Sometime after graduation, they decided to move in together. Drew was in law school while they were living together, and Liz was beginning her career.

Toward the end of his academic program, Drew's advisor told him that he was showing exceptional promise and that following school he should consider doing a clerkship. The clerkship would almost certainly require a move, but following one or two successful clerkships, Drew would have a competitive resume and be set up for a more promising career. All of this sounded appealing to Drew, an ambitious student who hoped to provide well for his future family as well as reach his full potential in his career.

Drew decided this was a good time to lay out a timeline to marry Liz. As he discussed his timeline with Liz — get engaged and married before the clerkship, and then move together, as a married couple, for the clerkship — Liz objected. She had no intentions of ever leaving the state they currently lived in, where both of their families lived. And while Drew attempted to explain they could come back, but that this was a good move for his career and for their future as a family, Liz still found reason to protest.

The writing was on the wall for Drew: Liz wasn't as committed to the relationship as he was. She was still thinking as an "I" and not as a "we." The result was Drew scratching his head wondering how they had dated for so long and not known this. Of course now he was stuck in a lease and a living situation with a woman with whom he had no future.

Researchers like Dr. Meg Jay, a psychologist and professor at the University of Virginia, would call Drew and Liz's situation the classic "sliding, not deciding" approach to relationships.[21] "Moving from dating to sleeping over to sleeping over a lot to cohabitation can be a gradual slope," Jay says, "one not marked by rings or ceremonies or sometimes even a conversation. Couples bypass talking about why they want to live together and what it will mean."

Thankfully for Drew and Liz, the realization they had different expectations for the future came before they got married instead of after. While the break-up of their relationship was complicated by the fact that they lived together, they didn't find themselves in a marriage in which one or both wanted out.

My generation, especially, is keen on the idea that living together before marriage is a good test of compatibility and a safeguard against divorce. We want to avoid the trauma of divorce we saw in our parents' generation, and our parents sometimes encourage cohabitating for the same reason. But, statistically, couples who live together before marriage and who are not engaged are more likely to divorce than couples who don't, according to the CDC.[22] That association may be stabilizing, according to the CDC, but other studies still show that marital satisfaction is less for couples who cohabitated than for those who didn't.

A study by the National Marriage Project indicated that couples who carry an "above average commitment" are less likely to divorce than their counterparts that don't carry such a high level of commitment.[23] The study defined "above average commitment" as the following:

- The extent to which spouses see their relationship in terms of "we" versus "me"

- The importance they attach to their relationship

- Their conviction that a better relationship with someone else does not exist

- Their desire to stay in the relationship "no matter what rough times we encounter"

Living together before marriage works against these traits of "above average commitment." Living together like a married couple while remaining less committed than a married couple allows individuals to develop habits centered around non-commitment and lack of trust. These habits are not easily broken by an exchange of rings and "I dos."

In the case of my friends Drew and Liz, their "we versus me" mentality wasn't in-sync. They clearly weren't placing the same importance on the relationship, nor did they seem to share the desire to stick together in the "rough times" (like living in a new city). The result for Drew and Liz, if they had decided to marry, could likely have been a divorce later down the road.

Even so, the psychological toll of the breakup was heavy given the time they'd invested and the breakup costs (both financial and emotional) involved. Both parties, but Drew especially, were eager to end this relationship, heal, and start looking for another romantic partner. But the lease had more than a few months left and the cost to break it was steep. With few other options available, Drew and Liz were left coexisting in an apartment when they no longer even wanted to be around each other.

## The Importance of the "Getting to Know You" Phase

"Living together completely abbreviated the get-to-know-you process that dating before marriage is designed to accomplish," wrote *Verily* magazine contributor Sara Jane Panfil as she explained her own experience of living with her boyfriend. "The priority became maintaining the household peace instead of probing one another's souls."[24]

She continued:

> One evening, for example, it became apparent that he and I did not share the same values regarding working motherhood. I was completely aghast at the things he said to me that night; I felt like I had gotten the wind knocked out of me. Who was this man that I was living with and how could this be his expectations for our — my — future?
>
> But I didn't say anything. I had class the next day, dinner to clean up, homework to do, and I just could not face such a serious conversation with no place to retreat to in case it went poorly. In a non-cohabitating situation, I probably would have broken up with him right then — it was that bad — or at least taken time to seriously reevaluate our relationship. But I did neither

of those things. I told myself that I could maybe change his mind sometime in the future and left it there. We went to sleep that night as usual.

Sara Jane continued to live with this man and even moved with him to another city before their relationship completely fell apart. But why would she stay with a man whose expectations for the future didn't seem to align with hers?

"Living with Jake meant that, emotionally, it was easier for me to say yes to D.C. than it was for me to face the daunting prospect of separating from him," Sara Jane explained.

"I had given away most of my large possessions prior to moving in with him, my room in my old apartment had been rented out, and I had fallen out of touch with most of my friends over the course of our relationship. I would have had to completely start over."

Sara Jane's story is a classic example of what researchers say resembles consumer lock-in. "Lock-in is the decreased likelihood to search for, or change to, another option once an investment in something has been made," Jay explains: "The greater the setup costs, the less likely we are to move to another, even better, situation, especially when faced with switching costs, or the time, money, and effort it requires to make a change."[25]

In other words, couples stay in a relationship that may be satisfactory but not satisfying because a change "costs" too much or is too "risky."

"If Jake had asked me to marry him, instead of asking me to move to Washington," Sara Jane elaborated, "I would have said yes. But I would have made a huge mistake."

Marriage wouldn't have fixed many of their differences, and they probably would have had to face them later.

The fallout could have been even more catastrophic, she speculated.

## When "Happily Ever After" Isn't

"Living together before marriage seems to resemble taking a car for a test drive," says marriage and family expert Dr. Roback Morse.

Yet "here's the problem with the car analogy," Roback Morse explains, "the car doesn't have hurt feelings if the driver dumps it back at the used car lot and decides not to buy it. The analogy works great if you picture yourself as the driver. It stinks if you picture yourself as the car."

Take, for example, a story my mom relayed to me recently. An acquaintance was telling my mom about her adult daughter's current love life troubles. The woman explained that her daughter had been in a relationship with a man for the past year, yet when she asked her how she was feeling about the relationship her daughter admitted she wasn't over her previous boyfriend.

Now, she had dated the last guy for a long time, the woman explained, and they had lived together for several years. But the relationship ended more than a year ago, and she's seeing someone great now. "I just can't figure out why she isn't over him," she said to my mom.

"Well of course she isn't over him," my mother said. "Breaking up with him was essentially a divorce." They lived as a married couple, she explained, and while they may not have realized it, the break-up would bring emotional fallout similar to the pain accompanying a divorce. The woman was stunned — the thought had never occurred to her. And it probably didn't occur to her daughter prior to making the decision to move in with her boyfriend.

Often, the expectations of men and women in cohabitating situations are different. A recent study by sociologists Michael Pollard and Kathleen Mullan Harris, of the RAND Corporation, indicates that men report less commitment to their live-in girlfriend than women do to their live-in boyfriend. Seventy-four percent of women living with their boyfriends reported being "completely committed," compared to fifty-nine percent of men who reported the same response.[26] Researchers also say that women are often more hopeful that living together is the next step toward marriage, while men are more likely to see the relationship as a trial for marriage.[27]

## Going Against the Trend

"Cohabitation is here to stay," says University of Virginia's Meg Jay. While the trends may point that way, not everyone needs to follow suit. And certainly, among a generation in which over 80 percent say that having a lasting marriage is one of their life goals, now's the time to make a case to *not* live together before marriage.[28]

A friend of mine (I'll call her Carolina) has been married for a few years but says she regrets her decision to cohabit with her husband prior to their marriage. "On paper, [seeing] all the practical reasons of why [to live together], I couldn't argue not to," she said. Their decision to cohabit came from a good place — they wanted to save money, and they were already engaged, so what was the real harm, they thought. But living together was not the precursor to marriage that she thought it was going to be.

"We had all kinds of issues that we had to work out [once we were married] — just with communication, expectations, honesty, directions," Carolina explained. "[These] were not worked out when we were living together, [and] only worked out once we were married."

The issues reared their head in the first year of marriage and it became "either fix this marriage or divorce," she explained, and she was adamant that divorce was not an option. "It took the commitment of the marriage to work it out," she said. But it was much harder to do in the first year of marriage, especially because Carolina now realized she had needed more time alone to grow as a person than she had allowed herself before marrying.

"Everyone we knew, everyone around us, was living together," she explained. And though she was raised in a Catholic family, attended Catholic schools, and she and her fiancé attended weekly Sunday Mass together, at the time she didn't have the supporting reasons to not cohabit. She knew it was wrong according to her upbringing — but that rationale wasn't enough to outweigh the practical "benefits."

Like many of the Church's teachings on sexuality, cohabitation is not an easy topic for a Sunday homily — where most adult Catholics get their continued knowledge about the Church's teachings. It's also not an easy conversation even among family and friends, who'd often rather stay supportive and keep the peace than rock the boat on issues related to love, sex, and marriage. But contrary to what many think, my generation is open to conversation and guidance in regard to relationships. And there are convincing, even attractive, arguments to be made against cohabitation for the sake of happier, healthier relationships and marriages, something nearly all my peers aspire to.

Take, for example, a conversation I had with a male friend I knew in college. We hadn't seen each other in a while and, on reconnecting, we discussed mutual friends and the direction their lives had taken post college. We chatted about one couple we thought would for sure be married by now, but instead were living together. We agreed that it seemed like a weird step for their relationship. "Why not just get married?" we both thought.

My friend however, then said he would consider living with a woman if he was already engaged to her. It's true that the risk for divorce and other negative side effects of cohabitation diminish if cohabitation begins after engagement — because a commitment has already been made.

"But why?" I asked. "You've already made it that long."

My friend explained that, practically speaking, if one of their leases ended before the other person's, then it would probably just make the most sense, logistically. To which I responded, "Oh, I'd find a friend's couch or floor to sleep on before I lived with my boyfriend or fiancé."

My friend was surprised by my insistence on avoiding cohabitation even when marriage is imminent. "Why?" he probed.

"For starters, it totally kills anticipation of the wedding," I said. "Marriage is the uniting of two lives not just through the exchange of vows and rings, but in every single aspect. Spending the night together before that, and especially moving into an apartment together, really turns the wedding into something merely symbolic, instead of something actually life changing."

But further, I explained, "Marriage is really hard. It will require sacrifice. And what better way to prepare for the sacrifices of marriage than to give up some comfort prior to marriage."

He seemed to be listening more intently at this point.

"To me," I explained, "the decision to not live together before marriage, even in engagement, is really a test of how much convenience you're willing to give up for the sake of the other person, the relationship, and a better, stronger marriage."

My friend looked at me a little taken aback at my reasoning, "You know, I've never thought of it that way," he said, "but it makes a lot of sense."

It's a common complaint of marriage experts and young adults alike that today's dating scripts are so loose it's sometimes hard for young adults to see which path is best for happy, healthy relationships and marriages.

Of course, no marriage can be completely safeguarded from the ups and downs of life. Complete commitment to another person will be both beautiful and hard, sometimes at the same time. There will be a learning curve in nearly every marriage. And life has its way of throwing challenges we can't anticipate.

But it's also true that our contentment and happiness in love is often the result of choices we've made along the way. Living together before marriage may provide temporary convenience and financial relief, but not living together before marriage will help establish selflessness, self-control, and strength, both in the individuals and in the relationship. And that's the stuff that builds long-lasting marriages.

---

*Meg T. McDonnell is the Executive Director of the Chiaroscuro Institute, a nonprofit devoted to assisting lower-income Americans to relink sex, kids, and marriage. She was awarded a 2011 Robert Novak Journalism Fellowship. Her writing has been published in the* Washington Post, International Business Times, *MercatorNet, National Review Online, and other religious and secular outlets.*

Chapter 7

# Parenting Skills
## It's Not Rocket Science

By Thomas Lickona

For more than four decades, my work as a developmental psychologist has focused on helping parents and teachers develop good character in youth. For the most part, effective parenting is common sense — the wisdom of the ages. What makes parenting harder than ever, however, are the changes in the world in which we're raising kids.

Before laying out a parent's battle plan for combating an environment that's increasingly hostile to moral values, let me share a personal story illustrating one of the biggest challenges we now face as families — the sexual culture. We saw that culture change before our eyes as our kids were growing up. By the mid-seventies, with the sexual revolution in full swing, the TV heroes and heroines with whom kids identify had taken to sleeping around. Observable effects on children soon followed. In the early eighties, when our younger son Matthew was in sixth grade, he told us that many of the boys in his class had started to "go with" girls. A few weeks later, he mentioned that these boys and girls were stopping at a park on the way home from school to play "Truth or Dare" in the pine trees.

I asked him, "What's Truth or Dare?"

He explained that kids stood in a circle, and when your turn came, you could choose "truth" or "dare." If you chose "truth," you had to answer truthfully any question you were asked. If you chose "dare," you had to do the dare.

I asked for an example of a dare.

Matthew said, "Okay … um … I dare Brian to go to the center of the circle and French kiss Jennifer."

He hastened to reassure me, "I always choose truth, Dad!"

"Well, I'm glad to hear that," I said. "But even if you yourself aren't doing things like French kissing, just being there gives approval to the kids who are doing bad stuff." He agreed to hang out on the park's playground equipment with another kid when the group went into the pine trees.

A few weeks later, Matthew came home and said that several of the boys in his class had told him they were going to have sex with their girlfriends when they got into seventh grade.

"What did you say?" I asked.

"That you're not supposed to do that until you're married." I was relieved to know he had absorbed that family value. But he added, "They still say they don't see anything wrong with it, and they're going to do it."

The debate between Matthew and his friends about premarital sex went on for another couple of weeks. (I don't remember coaching him along the way, though in retrospect that would have helped him give some reasons for his stance.) Finally, he recounted a conversation with a boy we often saw at Sunday Mass with his parents, who, we felt sure, would have been shocked to learn that their eleven-year-old son was talking about having sex with his girlfriend. This kid said to Matthew: "If you're not supposed to have sex until you're married, then how come they never say that in church?" (That prompted me to write up my conversations with Matthew in a letter to our pastor asking for a little help from the pulpit.)

Matthew is now a dad with six kids of his own. In his spiritual memoir, *Swimming with Scapulars: True Confessions of a Young Catholic*, he makes it very clear that he's far from a saint, but he says he was a virgin until his wedding night. So, even in a toxic culture, there's reason to hope that a family's moral values — with parental effort, the grace of God, and children's willingness to cooperate with those helps — will take root in their conscience and character.

However, a societal environment that can't be counted on to support good character means parents have to be more vigilant, more intentional, than in past generations. In today's world, we have to take deliberate steps to create a strong family life that builds close relationships, teaches good values, fosters the faith, and fortifies our kids against the cultural temptations and pressures. The good news is that millions of couples who have embraced that challenge have found raising a family a deep source of meaning, fulfillment, and joy. Let's look at seven principles of parenting that can help to make it so.

## 1. Make Character Development a High Priority

Wise parents ask, "What kind of child do we want to raise, and how will we do it?"

A good way to answer that question is to sit down and write a "family touchstone." A touchstone expresses the values and virtues you want all family members, parents as well as kids, to feel accountable to and live by. When their four kids were young, Catholic parents Matt and Suzanne Davidson wrote the following touchstone that they hung in the kitchen, where they could review it at the start of the week and refer to it whenever they needed to:

<u>The Davidson Way</u>

- We commit to being honest and trustworthy, kind, and fair. We don't lie, cheat, steal, or intentionally hurt others.

- We don't whine, complain, or make excuses.

- When we make a mistake, we make up for it, learn from it, and move on.

- We work to keep our minds, bodies, and souls healthy, strong, and pure.

- We commit to learning and growing in our faith through practice and trust in God's goodness.

- We live with an attitude of gratitude and joy.

Another family we know had an embroidered sign hanging in their home: *"Remember you're a Morfit."* A simple reminder, aimed at keeping kids identified with the family values.

If we're going to emphasize character with our kids, we need a clear concept of what it is. Good character consists of virtues. Virtues are good habits — inner dispositions, developed through practice, to behave in morally good ways.

What are the human virtues needed to be a person of character? Here are ten affirmed by nearly all cultural and religious traditions:

- *Wisdom* — good judgment, knowing right from wrong
- *Justice* — respecting the rights, dignity, and worth of all persons
- *Fortitude* — the "inner toughness" that enables us to do what's right in the face of difficulty
- *Self-control* — the ability to govern our appetites, impulses, and emotions
- *Love* — being kind, compassionate, generous, and forgiving
- *Hard work* — doing our best no matter what we do
- *Positive attitude* — finding the good in all situations
- *Integrity* — being true to ourselves and standing up for what's right
- *Gratitude* — thanking God and others for our blessings and not complaining
- *Humility* — knowing our strengths and weaknesses and striving to be a better person

We should help kids recognize their virtues ("That was generous of you to share with your sister.") and their areas for growth ("How can you work on controlling that temper? Let's make a plan."). And we should make it clear that we're also trying to be better people — that our character, like theirs, is a work in progress.

## 2. Love Your Children

Dozens of studies show that a warm, caring, and responsive parent-child relationship is strongly linked to children's healthy development. When kids feel loved, they become attached to us. That attachment makes them receptive to our values.

What does it mean to love our children? We do that by taking care of them: meeting their physical and emotional needs; showing affection; taking the long view, considering how our actions will affect the kind of person they are becoming; affirming them in authentic ways; showing interest in their lives and respecting them as individuals; spending time together; having meaningful communication; and sacrificing for them. Let me illustrate just some of these ways of making parental love real and felt in our relationships with our children.

### Taking the Long View

In my graduate course on character education, I asked my students to write an essay on the question, "How did your parents affect your character development?" A young woman in her early twenties wrote this poignant response:

> I was an only child, and my parents knowingly let me have my way most of the time to show how much they loved me. But the long-term effect on me is that I have struggled with selfishness my whole life. I'm used to getting my own way, and when someone goes against me, I take it very personally.

The Catholic educator James Stenson, in his book *Compass: A Handbook on Parent Leadership*, says that effective parents "see themselves as raising adults. They view their children as adults-in-the-making." That means asking: What will my kids be like when they are grown men and women? Will they be hardworking and responsible? Will they make loving husbands and wives and capable mothers and fathers? How might my actions now as a parent affect those outcomes?

### Affirmation

In his book *Healing the Unaffirmed,* the Catholic psychotherapist Conrad Baars says that many of the patients he sees suffer from "emotional deprivation disorder." They struggle with feelings of being unloved and unlovable, oversensitive, insecure and afraid of life, depressed, and unable to make friends and relate to others. These feelings, Baars believes, stem from not receiving enough loving affirmation — and often getting far too much criticism — when they were growing up in their families.

Affirmation can be as simple as, "Thanks for doing the dishes — the kitchen looks great!" or a note in a kid's lunch bag: "Andy, have a good day at school. I love you. Dad." Or it can be a treasured family tradition, such as "The Christmas Love Letter" written by our friends John and Kathy Colligan. Kathy explains:

> Each Christmas, my husband John and I would write a letter to each of our five kids and put it under the tree. We'd tell them what we loved and appreciated about them, the ways we'd seen them grow during the past year, the talents and character strengths we saw emerging, all the things we cherished. It was always the last present they opened, and the one that meant the most to them.

### Together Time

One study asked adults to relate their favorite childhood memories. People typically remembered not expensive toys, clothes, or trips, but the simple things they did with their parents or as a family: playing board games, taking walks, playing catch, going swimming or fishing, outings for ice cream, tenting overnight in the backyard.

### Meaningful Communication

Christian Barnard, originator of the heart transplant, recalled Sunday afternoon walks and talks with his father. They'd hike to the top of the hill by the dam, sit on a rock, and look down at the town below. "Then I would tell my problems to my father, and he would speak of his to me." This kind of one-on-one, emotionally intimate communication is especially important for building the bonds that give parents the inside track in a world of competing influences.

As a Catholic father once said, we should also "make a big deal of the family meal." That time is potentially an island of intimacy for sharing experiences, beliefs, and values. To make conversation meaningful and get everyone talking, it helps to have a topic: What was the best part and the hardest part of your day? What was something you learned today, in school or just from life? What's a way you helped someone, or someone helped you? What are you grateful for today? (For more family conversation starters, see the 2013 issue of *excellence & ethics*, our character education newsletter, at www.cortland.edu/character.)

### Love as Sacrifice

One young woman, now a Sister of Life, says:

> The language of my father's love was the sacrifices he made to be with his family. He was home for dinner every night, helped my mother with the cooking, and was always the last to sit down. Evenings were often spent helping us with our homework, weekends going to our games. His gentle encouragement helped me when I was struggling in school or sports. In re-

ceiving his love, I found that I not only wanted to love him, but I wanted to be good for him.

For many parents, there is no greater sacrifice than to endure the inevitable trials and sufferings of marriage. Says one mother: "The most important thing parents can do for their children is to love each other and stay together."

## 3. Exercise Authority Wisely

A friend from Australia says that since coming to the U.S., he has often witnessed the following scene: A parent he's talking with tells his or her child to do something. The child ignores the directive, says something disdainful like, "Yeah, right," and walks away. The parent then gestures helplessly to my Australian friend and says, "What can you do with a kid like that?"

Parents must have a strong sense of their moral authority — of having the right to be respected and obeyed. In *The Moral Child*, Stanford psychologist William Damon states that how well parents teach their child to respect their authority lays the foundation for future moral growth. In *Take Back Your Kids*, Catholic family psychologist William Doherty says that we face "an epidemic of insecure parenting." Insecure parents, he says, are skittish about exercising parental authority, refuse ever to get angry with their kids, and consequently allow their kids to walk all over them.

Occasional, non-abusive parental anger is necessary, as Doherty points out, particularly when kids are blatantly disrespectful or defiant. In the scenario above, described by my Australian friend, an appropriate parental response to the kid's contemptuous public disobedience would have been to take him by the collar, march him off to a private place, and say to him eye-to-eye: "Look, buster, I'm your mother. You don't talk to me like that — not at home, not in public, not ever. If you know what's good for you, you will do what I said — *immediately*."

Fortunately, there's solid research showing why and how to exercise parental authority. Berkeley psychologist Diana Baumrind observed families in their homes and identified three styles of parenting: *authoritative, authoritarian,* and *permissive.* Authoritarian parents used lots of commands and threats but little reasoning. Permissive parents were high on affection but low on authority. By contrast, *authoritative* parents combined confident authority with reasoning, fairness, love, and encouragement of age-appropriate self-reliance. At all developmental levels, Baumrind's research and other studies have shown that authoritative parents have the most secure, competent, and morally responsible kids.

In practice, authoritative parenting means at least five things.

First, we must take strong stands that are consistent with our values. For example, do we prohibit TV shows, movies, and video games that contain sex, graphic violence, or foul language; music with profane, lewd, or denigrating lyrics; all forms of pornography; immodest dress; parties where there's drinking; prom overnights? And do we explain to kids the reason for our rules, so they understand they're not arbitrary, but based on our love and concern for their welfare?

Second, we must have a zero tolerance policy for any kind of disrespectful back-talk, paying attention to both tone and content. When kids cross the line into disrespect, they need immediate, sometimes sharp corrective feedback, such as "What is your tone of voice?" or "You are not allowed to speak to me in that way, even when you're upset."

Third, we must make wise use of all the teachable moments presented by children's transgressions. Even small things — a mean remark to a sibling, a minor lie, a failure to do an assigned chore — should be taken seriously. Over time, dealing with the small stuff will have a cumulative effect on our child's conscience. If we let little things go, there won't be a foundation for dealing with bigger problems later on. If we don't correct rudeness in a six-year-old, we'll have trouble reigning in swearing and door-slamming by a sixteen-year-old.

Fourth, we should discipline in a way that gets kids to take responsibility for their actions. One way to do that is to make them their own judge and jury: "What do you think is a fair consequence for what you did?" Whenever possible, we should require restitution: "What can you do to make up for it?" If kids say, "I don't know," give them a choice of two things they could do to heal a hurt, restore family peace, help around the house, and so forth.

Finally, the wise exercise of parental authority requires vigilant supervision. The research on authoritative parents describes such parents as knowing where their kids are, who they're with, and what they're doing, including their online activity. These hands-on parents have teens with the lowest rates of sexual activity and drug and alcohol abuse. Meg Meeker, M.D., author of books such as *Strong Fathers, Strong Daughters* and *Your Kids at Risk: How Teen Sex Threatens Our Sons and Daughters*, gives this advice to parents: "Watch your kids like a hawk."

If you haven't established this kind of authoritative parenting style, you may need to give your child what I call the "obedience speech" (ideally when they're little, but it's never too late). In a quiet moment, explain:

There's something very important we want you to understand: mothers and fathers have the job of being in charge of the family. God gives us that responsibility. Kids have the job of *obeying* their parents — doing what we ask you to do. It's the same in school: A teacher is in charge of the classroom. Kids have to do what the teacher says.

So when we ask you to do something — come to dinner, pick up your toys, get ready for bed — you have to obey. You can't say, "No." That's not allowed. If you forget, we'll give you one reminder: *"Remember our talk about obedience."* If you continue to disobey, then there will have to be a consequence.

And we'd like you to obey *cheerfully*, without complaining. Obeying cheerfully makes the family a happier place for everybody.

Okay, can you tell me what I said? (Patiently review whatever needs repeating.)

The big idea we want to teach our kids is that obedience is a virtue. As David Isaacs points out in his book *Character Building*, "Children should be encouraged to obey not primarily out of fear — a low-level motive — but out of love, to help their parents. Obedience is the first step toward developing the virtue of generosity."

## 4. Teach By Example

Teaching by example includes treating our children with love and respect, but it goes well beyond that. One mother describes some of the many things her parents did that are etched in her memory:

My parents weren't perfect, but they were respectful of one another and supported each other in their childrearing decisions. No one in our family cursed. My mother was always helping out others in the community. My father showed tremendous kindness toward people and animals. Both of my parents were really interested in how people lived in past generations and in different cultures, and they fostered our understanding of that. They would also frequently voice their opinions about societal issues.

Many kids would have trouble answering the question, "What do your parents stand for?" If you've ever taken a stand in the workplace, participated in a protest, written a letter to the editor, or expressed a strong conviction that went against what others were saying, have you shared that, and your moral reasoning, with your children? Stands like these define your values and model moral courage.

We increase the power of our own example when we expose our children to other positive role models. The Giraffe Heroes Project (www.giraffe.org) has developed a bank of more than a thousand stories of everyday heroes of all ages who have shown compassion and courage by sticking out their necks for others. William Kilpatrick's *Books That Build Character* provides an annotated bibliography of hundreds of fiction and non-fiction books whose admirable characters will live in a young person's imagination. The website www.teachwithmovies.com catalogs hundreds of good films that offer positive role models and strong character themes. And we should be sure to tap the rich resource provided by the lives of the saints (see Mary Reed Newland's excellent book *The Saints and Our Children*).

# 5. Teach Directly

If we want to maximize the positive impact of our example, our kids need to know the values and beliefs that lie behind it. We need to practice what we preach, but we also need to preach what we practice.

Moral heroes — people who rescued Jews from the Holocaust, for example — have described their parents as both modeling and explicitly teaching high moral standards. For example, one rescuer said, "My mother always said to do some good for someone at least once a day."

We can start by directly teaching everyday manners: "Say please and thank you." "Don't interrupt someone who's speaking." "Look at a person who's talking to you." "Clear your dishes from the table." Hundreds of small teachings like these communicate to children, "This is how we behave, this is how we live."

Direct teaching includes explaining why some things are right and others wrong. Why is it wrong to be unkind — to call names, bully, or exclude others? Because you wouldn't want to be treated that way. Because when you do those things, it creates an "inside hurt" for the other person. You can't see it, but it hurts more, and often lasts longer, than an "outside hurt" that you can see. Why is it wrong to lie? Because lying destroys trust, and trust is the basis of any relationship.

We should also directly teach the fundamentals of our faith, starting with the three purposes of our lives: *salvation* (getting to heaven and helping others get there), *service* (using our gifts to build God's kingdom here on earth), and *holiness* (growing closer to God and becoming more like Jesus). We should make a list of other Catholic truths we want to teach our children, for example:

- There is such a thing as truth. We're Catholic because we believe what the Church teaches is true. Jesus promised to send the Holy Spirit, the source of all truth, to guide the Church when it teaches about faith and morals.

- Life is sacred, from conception until natural death. We must respect and defend it.

- We have a special duty to help Christ's "least ones" — the poor, homeless, disabled, sick, oppressed, and unborn.

- Sex is the beautiful gift of a good God, but he reserves it for the marriage of a husband and wife.

## 6. Solve Conflicts Fairly

Conflicts — between parents and kids or kids and each other — are an unavoidable part of family life. They can lead to a build-up of tension, explosions of yelling and screaming, and a residue of anger and alienation. But handled in the right way, conflicts can make a family stronger, teach kids responsibility for helping to create a happy family, and develop listening and problem-solving skills they can use throughout their lives.

In my work with parents, I've encouraged them to have sit-down family meetings weekly, or as needed, to address the issues that cause conflicts. Here's my eight-step recipe for a successful family meeting:

1. Choose a practical problem, such as morning hassles, bedtime battles, kids not getting along — perhaps a problem that was a source of tension during the previous week.

2. In the days before your first family meeting, lay the groundwork that will help it be a positive experience, not an exchange of accusations or put-downs. Have at least a brief individual conversation with each family member. See how they feel about the problem. Explain that the purpose of the family meeting will be to "find a solution that's fair to everyone." Set a time to meet. However, if the time arrives and the family atmosphere isn't good, postpone the meeting.

3. Start the family meeting with a prayer. To create a flow of positive feelings, do a quick round of what our family called Appreciation Time: "What's something that someone in the family did for you lately that you appreciated?"

4. Then set ground rules for discussion. Give everybody a voice in that. Ask, "What rules will help us have respectful talking and listening?" (Examples: "One person speaks at a time." "Look at and listen to the person who's talking.")

5. Emphasize again that the purpose of a family meeting is *cooperative problem-solving*, not blaming. "Let's have a *positive* discussion where everybody helps to solve the problem. Please express your feelings in a nice way." (Expect to have to remind kids of this during the meeting.)

6. Go around the table, giving everyone a chance to express a point of view. Write down proposed solutions. Discuss those and combine them into an agreed-upon plan.

7. Keep the meeting's pace brisk and, ideally, under half an hour.

8. Sign and post your Family Agreement — including when you'll meet again to discuss how it's working and what changes, if any, are needed to make it work better.

It will take some practice for family meetings to feel natural and go smoothly. But stick with it, and you'll reap the rewards. Studies have found that over time, these problem-solving sessions make for more cooperative kids and happier, less stressful households.

## 7. Provide Authentic Experiences of the Faith

Research has found that youth who frequently attend religious services and say their faith is important to them exhibit lower levels of sexual activity and drug and alcohol use, and higher levels of altruistic attitudes and behaviors.

How can we foster the kind of faith that is not just professed but lived out in everyday life? One Catholic family had a tradition of a partial fast every Monday night (broth for the parents, a piece of fruit for the kids) and sending the money saved to Catholic Relief Services. A Catholic father found that volunteering with his self-centered fifteen-year-old son at the city's soup kitchen got the son thinking less about the latest stuff he wanted and more about the needs of others. Service gives us a chance to remind our kids of what Jesus said: When we care for his "least ones," we are loving Christ himself.

Catholics who want the faith to take root in their kids make sure they not only get to Mass but also go to Confession. Confession requires us to examine our conscience, tell

God we're sorry for our sins, and resolve to do better. We encounter Jesus and experience his forgiveness.

But why do so many kids raised in families of faith, even those that practice regularly, fall away when they leave home? The late Father Hugh Thwaites said that in his experience, there are three reasons. The first is sin. "Before there is a spiritual falling away, there is usually a moral falling away."

The second reason is that the young person "never personally grasped the meaning of the faith." Religion was just a set of external behaviors. The third reason is linked with the second: The young person did not have a personal prayer life. "The absence of any prayer life," Father Thwaites said, "will so weaken the spiritual life that it will be unable to meet the onslaughts of a pagan world. What food and drink is to the body, prayer is to the soul."

How can we help our kids develop the habit of personal prayer? Our beloved Monsignor Minehan, before God took him home, would tell the teens in our parish preparing for Confirmation to give God just two minutes, two quiet minutes, at the start of the day. Don't fake it, he said. Talk to God as if he's right there — which, of course, he is. ("God, there's this kid at school … I'd like to rearrange his face. What should I do?") And then shut up and listen. As Mother Teresa said, "God speaks to us in the silence of our hearts."

If kids draw close to God in prayer, they will usually find that God draws close to them. Here's a high school boy:

> Before, I didn't even think about God. I never prayed. But when you're a teenager, you face a lot of problems. Now I believe that, basically, you need God. You can always go to him. When you pray, your problem

might not get fixed when you want, or the way you want, but you will get help.

So teach your kids to pray. Let them see you pray, pray with them, pray over them, and pray for them. And talk to them about when, why, and how you pray.

And yet, even after developing a prayer relationship with God, we can still fall away. To keep the elements of a close relationship with God always in mind, our family has an index card on the refrigerator that lists the "5 Ingredients of the Spiritual Life":

- Mental and vocal prayer
- The Mass and the sacraments
- Spiritual reading
- Self-denial
- Good works

During the college years and beyond, when the surrounding environment may be hostile to faith, spiritual reading becomes especially important. For my wife Judy and me, the works of C.S. Lewis, in the early years of our marriage, got us started on the path of reading good spiritual books. Ralph Martin's *Hungry for God* introduced me to the notion of seeking "intimacy with God." If our kids don't get such books for themselves, we can include them among their presents on Christmas and birthdays.

A caveat in closing: There is not a one-to-one correspondence between our efforts as parents and the choices our children will make, now or in the future. But while we don't control the person our child becomes, we should take to heart the advice of an old rabbi: "The worst mistake parents can make is to underestimate their influence." God gives us countless opportunities to help our children grow in goodness and to come to know, love, and serve him. We must do all we can, with the help of his grace, to aid them on that journey.

Yes, it's hard work (maybe not rocket science), but no work is more worthwhile.

---

*Thomas Lickona is director of the Center for the 4th & 5th Rs (www.cortland.edu/character) and professor of education emeritus at the State University of New York at Cortland. He is author or editor of eight books on character development in families and schools, including* Raising Good Children, Character Matters, *and, with his wife Judy and William Boudreau, M.D., a book for teens,* Sex, Love, and You: Making the Right Decision.

# Chapter 8

# *Having Hope for Marriage as a Child of Divorce*

By Joseph D. White, Ph.D.

I was recently talking with my fifteen-year-old goddaughter about her future, and I said something that began with, "If you get married and have kids someday…." She quickly interjected, "I'm *never* going to get married." Surprised and somewhat taken aback I asked, "Why not?" "It causes too many problems," she replied. My goddaughter's point of view is, unfortunately, not uncommon in teens and young adults today. There's skepticism about marriage, a sense that it's more trouble than it's worth, and a fear that it will only lead to disaster.

Perhaps that's why marriage rates are declining so drastically. In July of 2013, the National Center for Marriage and Family Research released a study showing that the marriage rate in the United States is now 31.1. This means that each year, out of one thousand unmarried women in the U.S., only 31 decide to say, "I do." This is a historic low, only about one-third of the marriage rate ninety years ago. Why the decline? As a child of divorce, I think I know.

## Divorce and the Fear of Commitment

The sexual revolution of the sixties and seventies brought many things never before seen in our society, including widespread contraception, casual sex, and an alarming increase in rates of divorce. In 1980, shortly after my own parents divorced, the U.S. divorce rate was at its peak — 22.6 divorces per year for every 1000 married women.

When my parents separated, I had no idea what was happening. I tried to get used to going back and forth between Mom's house and Dad's house, but what I really wanted was for everyone to be in the same place. Both my mom and dad found someone new, and I gave up hope of seeing them together again. But I still resented living in two worlds, especially when that meant passing messages back and forth.

I also remember carrying around a sense of shame — not necessarily because I felt like the divorce was my fault, but just because I felt like my family was somehow "less than" others. As I grew older, I wondered what my own experience of marriage would be. I approached relationships with distrust, and I feared being abandoned.

My experiences were not uncommon. In 2005, University of Texas sociology professor Norvall Glenn and Elizabeth Marquardt from the Institute for American Values released a landmark study on adult children of divorced parents. Their study is summarized in the book *Between Two Worlds: The Inner Lives of Children of Divorce*. The study surveyed 1500 young adults from across the country, half from divorced families and half from intact ones. The project is unique in both scope and focus. While previous studies (usually with smaller and less diverse samples) had focused primarily on external outcomes of children of divorce (for example, rates of incarceration, academic and occupational achievement, and so forth), the study by Glenn and Marquardt focused primarily on the differences in attitudes, thoughts, and feelings between young adults whose parents stayed married and those who came from divorced families.

The results were striking: Divorce has a profound effect on the identities of children. Forced to live in two separate worlds — the world of the mother and the world of the father — they often feel like two different people living in the same body. And the effort to shield children from the pain of divorce — to separate as amicably as possible — does little to help. Children from "good" divorces still feel a great deal of conflict about their parents' separation; it's just more difficult to make sense of the conflict because it is more internal than external.

In fact, when divorced parents continue to act as friendly co-parents, their children can't blame mother or father for the divorce, so they often blame marriage itself. Adult children of divorce in general, and children of amicable divorces in particular, have a more negative view of marriage than do their peers from intact families.

This might explain, at least in part, why so many young adults today hesitate to make the commitment to marriage. We see evidence of this in the high rates of cohabitation among couples today. A recent report from the Centers for Disease Control and Prevention showed that nearly half of women were not married to their spouse or partner when they first lived with them. Beyond the moral implications of cohabitation (which is no small issue), there is also a practical concern: cohabiting couples who go on to get married are more likely to divorce — much more likely. Empirical studies show that couples who lived together prior to marriage are 40–85 percent more likely to get divorced.

This was somewhat of a mystery to social scientists until Dr. Scott Stanley and his team at the Center for Marital and Family Studies at the University of Denver (Stanley et al., 2004) helped shed light on the issue. Stanley and colleagues found that couples who live together prior to marriage often do so because they aren't fully ready to make the commitment to marry. This may or may not be about the partner they have chosen. Sometimes they are unsure about him or her, but other times it is their past experience with marriage (such as being the child of divorce) that has made them uneasy about making the commitment.

The problem is, these couples tend to have lower levels of commitment to their partners even *after* marriage, leading to higher divorce rates. This challenges the cultural folk wisdom that living together is a good way to see if you are compatible with your partner — a form of trial marriage or "marriage insurance." In fact, research would indicate that cohabitation is exactly the opposite — a risk factor that a couple will continue to be less committed to one another and eventually separate.

I was raised in a conservative evangelical Protestant family, and my wife was raised Catholic. We didn't live together before marriage because it just wouldn't have been proper according to our upbringing. But that doesn't mean I didn't have a great deal of anxiety about getting married. In fact, I had what was probably the biggest migraine of my life on our wedding day. The commitment to marriage felt so daunting in part because of the painful divorce I had witnessed as a child. When my wife and I first started talking about marriage, I said, "Let's make a deal that if we get married, divorce won't ever be part of the conversation. It will never be an option."

And the rest is history. We've been married now for nineteen years. Like all marriages, it's been challenging at times, but we've stuck it out "in good times and in bad." We've also learned some things along the way about what keeps people together. Some of the following recommendations are things we did, others are things we wish we had done (or done *sooner*).

Most of all, I want engaged and married couples to know there is *hope* for marriage. It takes work, but happy marriages are possible. What makes them possible is no longer a mystery. The past few decades of research in the social sciences has told us a great deal about what makes marriages happy, and you'll see some of that here as well.

## Secrets to Marital Success in an Age of Divorce

### *Make the Marriage Sacramental*

Matthew and Lindsey were married in a civil ceremony before a justice of the peace. Even though Lindsey was raised Catholic and Matthew grew up Baptist, both had stopped going to church in college, and they didn't see much point to going to a church for a wedding ceremony. But when Lindsey came back to the Catholic Church five years later, she wanted the marriage to be Catholic as well. Fortunately, Matthew was amenable to this, and he started going to Mass with Lindsey and then began the RCIA inquiry.

They discussed their situation with a priest and, after working out the details, were able to establish a sacramental marriage in a process known as convalidation. Six months later, Matthew and Lindsey spoke about the difference it made. "We had a good marriage, but it became a *great* one," Matthew said. "We were connected in so many ways — emotionally, mentally, and physically. But adding this spiritual dimension to our relationship made us even closer." Lindsey agreed. "The grace of marriage is real," she said. "I have grown in patience and in love. I never thought I could feel this close to another person."

Many couples still get married in a church, others don't. But for a Catholic, sacramental marriage means more than a prayer prayed over the bride and groom. In our Faith, a sacrament is a visible sign of an invisible spiritual reality. Not just a symbol, in a sacrament the sign contains what it signifies. The visible sign in baptism is the pouring of (or immersion in) water. In marriage, it is the exchange of vows between the man and woman. What is the reality they signify? There are actually two: the relationship between Christ and his Church (see Ephesians 5:21–33); and the communion of persons found in the Holy Trinity.

From the very beginning, God created us male and female:

> So God created man in his own image, in the image of God he created him; male and female he created them. (Genesis 1:27)

Humans are created male and female "in the divine image," meaning that there is something about being made male and female that images God himself. As a spiritual being, God does not have gender, so it's not male-ness or female-ness that images God, but it is the complementarity of the sexes. Jesus gives us insight into this when he says the following:

> Have you not read that he who made them from the beginning made them male and female, and said, "For

this reason a man shall leave his father and mother and be joined to his wife, and the two shall become one"? So they are no longer two but one. (Matthew 19:4–6)

## Avoid Cohabitation

Cami and Steve met through mutual friends and dated off and on during their freshman and sophomore years of college. Eventually, they began to see each other exclusively. They were sexually active throughout the relationship and spent some nights together, usually at Cami's apartment because Steve had a roommate. Eventually, as Steve stayed over more often, he had a drawer in Cami's dresser and a small space in the closet. When Steve's roommate was about to graduate, Steve and Cami agreed that it didn't make sense for Steve to try to keep the apartment alone, since he was spending more time at Cami's place anyway. Cami invited Steve to move in with her, and he agreed.

After living together about eighteen months, Cami and Steve decided to "make it official." Cami's parents, especially, had been pressing her about whether or not the relationship was going to proceed to marriage. "Why not?" Steve and Cami asked themselves. They were mostly living like a married couple anyway.

According to the research, individuals who live together before marriage often get caught up in a sort of "relationship inertia" in which getting married is just the next logical step. They are less likely to make a conscious, intentional decision to commit to their partner for life. Those who are currently living together before marriage should discern whether they can make an objective, intentional decision to commit to this person for life. This will help reduce the chances of going the way of the statistics.

In order to be really objective about this, the couple might need to make separate living arrangements, or at least abstain from sexual activity prior to the marriage. (As we all know, our hormones can sometimes keep us from thinking clearly!) Couples should ask themselves, "Would I choose to marry this person, and commit to him (or her) for the rest of my life, even if our lives weren't already tied together by living arrangements and history? If the answer is "yes," then go forward. If the answer is "no," backing out now, no matter how painful, will save a great deal of pain in the future.

### Practice Pre-Martial and Marital Chastity

Karen and John grew up very differently. John was raised by liberal parents who came of age in the seventies era of "free love." They encouraged him to go after his passions, whether they be life goals or cute girls. They even supplied him with condoms when he was a teen, saying that they didn't mind him having sex, but they *did* want to make sure he kept himself "safe." Karen, on the other hand, was raised by strict, very religious parents whom she described as overprotective. Under her parents "watchful eyes," she was rarely even alone with a boy, much less doing anything sexual.

John and Karen married when he was twenty and she was barely eighteen. Karen was still a virgin on their wedding night, which John said he thought was "sweet." Karen, however, felt some insecurity about her lack of experience and also wondered if John might be comparing her with other girls he had slept with. For his part, John found the transition to "perpetual monogamy" difficult. Although he didn't have sex with other women, he struggled with a wandering eye, both in daily life and on the Internet.

In the marriage vows, we give ourselves as free, total, and exclusive gifts to our spouses. Our bodies confirm this in the sexual act. In the language of the body, making love says, "I give myself completely to you." It doesn't make sense to say this with our bodies unless we really have given ourselves to each other in a covenant relationship. Why? Because couples engaging in premarital sex can always walk away from one another. Even though they might be saying, "I give myself to you" with their bodies, they can go their separate ways. In contrast, couples in a valid sacramental marriage are joined to one another for life; the two have become one. Couples who wait until after marriage to have sex are 29–47 percent more likely to enjoy sex during marriage, according to a study by Hering (1994).

Self-giving love is also evidenced in faithfulness between spouses. Major hurt and disruption to relationships is caused by extramarital affairs, viewing of pornography, and "emotional affairs" (in which one spouse invests him or herself emotionally in someone else, rationalizing the relationship because it is not a sexual one). While marriages in which these things happen usually are troubled prior to the affair, unfaithfulness can push the relationship to the breaking point, causing lasting wounds that may not heal.

### Keep the Faith!

Part of what made Matthew and Lindsey's marriage grow when Lindsey returned to the Church and Matthew became Catholic was the ongoing experience of faith. As each of them grew closer to God and to his Church, they also naturally grew closer to one another in a way they hadn't anticipated. They agreed that this made their marriage stronger than they thought possible.

Research suggests that couples who attend church weekly are less likely to divorce. Also, couples should spend time together in prayer. Pope John Paul II, in his *Letter to Families*, writes, "Prayer increases the strength and spiritual unity of the family, helping the family to partake of God's own 'strength'" (*Letter to Families*, 4). Many couples, however, have limited experience of praying together. If you are in this situation, consider using a combination of traditional and spontaneous prayer. Traditional prayers are the pre-written, memorized prayers we sometimes recite in church so we are able to speak to God with one voice. Spontaneous prayer is speaking to God in our own words.

A good way to begin spontaneous prayer is to review the forms of prayer mentioned in the *Catechism* and try to spend a little time on each form of prayer. For example, thank God for some specific things he has done in your life, pray for family members and friends who need God's help, and then bring your own requests to God. You can take turns on these forms of prayer, and then close with a traditional prayer, such as the Our Father.

You might also wish to pray silently together, perhaps before the Blessed Sacrament at church. Other ideas include taking turns reading the Psalms to one another or praying the Rosary together. Try a few different ways to pray together and continue those that feel most natural and enriching to your relationship with God and one another.

### Use Natural Family Planning

Like many couples, Rob and Marisa knew Church teaching on contraception, but it didn't make sense to them. Why should they let the Church dictate how they regulated their family size? They felt that not using artificial contraception was too much of a risk. At first, they wanted to wait until they felt financially secure enough to support a family before having a child. Once they decided to go ahead, it took longer than they expected to get pregnant, but they had one, and then two children.

They had just decided that Marisa would go back on the Pill now that they had the two children they wanted. Then they attended a talk on the Theology of the Body at their local parish. Once they heard the rationale behind the Church's teaching, they felt conflicted. Finally, they decided together to attend a class on Natural Family Planning. They were pleasantly surprised, both with the science behind the method and with the practical way it could be applied.

The biggest surprise, however, was the impact on their marriage. "We started feeling closer to one another, communicating better," said Rob. "When you talk about even the most personal things, like what is happening with your body," Marisa said, "you feel like you can talk about anything."

Couples who are married in the Catholic Church promise, as part of the marriage rite, to be open to children from God. This openness to life means working with the natural fertility God gave us, instead of against it, even if the couple prayerfully discerns that there are grave reasons to postpone pregnancy. Natural Family Planning, or NFP, is a term used to describe various methods of learning about and keeping track of a woman's fertility cycles and using this information to achieve or postpone pregnancy.

Studies by many different researchers, including the U.S. Department of Health, Education, and Welfare, the World Health Organization, Fairfield University, and others, have indicated a 94 to 99 percent effectiveness rate for NFP, depending on the method chosen, provided that couples use the method appropriately.

NFP also has other advantages. Many couples who use NFP say that it helps them be "more in tune with one another," to communicate better and to better understand one another's needs. In fact, a Michigan State University study showed higher levels of marital satisfaction among couples who use NFP versus other methods of family planning, and some studies have indicated that the rate of divorce for couples who practice NFP is extremely low — between 0.6 percent and 4.2 percent.

### Practice Effective Conflict Resolution

When I asked my grandparents what advice they had for married couples, after fifty-nine years of marriage, they didn't hesitate. "Keep the list of grudges as short as possible," my grandfather said. My grandmother agreed. "Most things couples argue about just aren't that important. That is, at least, it won't be important later. If it's not something you will care about a few days after the fact, why argue about it now?" But not all disagreements can be avoided or easily dismissed. "When there is something important," my grandfather added, "talk about it. Make sure you talk about it calmly and get it worked out as soon as possible."

Chances are that individuals who are children of divorce saw many examples during childhood of poor conflict-resolution skills between spouses. But there are healthy ways to deal with disagreements. A healthy marriage is not one that is free of conflict. In fact, researchers have found no relationship between the number or frequency of disagreements and marital dissatisfaction. Some happy couples have lots of conflicts, and some unhappy ones have very few. What makes the difference between happy and unhappy couples is how conflicts are resolved once they occur. By using sensitive, healthy communication skills, a couple can work through conflicts and make their marriage stronger.

One key is to practice empathy and forgiveness. When you are angry or dismayed by what your spouse is doing or saying, try to imagine yourself in his or her shoes. Work toward forgiveness and trust when hurts occur. Grudges can devastate a marriage, but choosing to let go of angry feelings gives us the freedom to go on.

## Hope for Marriage

Children of divorce, like me, have experienced the great pain of marriages gone wrong. But there is hope for marriage. Our hope lies in this: God is the author of marriage. It was part of his plan from the very beginning. And God does not call us to something that is destined to fail. The Bible tells us, "For I know the plans I have for you, says the LORD, plans for welfare and not for evil, to give you a future and a hope" (Jeremiah 29:11). Have hope for marriage. When it happens according to God's plan, it will surely succeed.

---

*Joseph D. White, Ph.D., is a practicing clinical psychologist, national catechetical consultant, and the author of numerous books, including* A Catholic Parent's Tool Box: Raising Healthy Children in the 21st Century.

# Chapter 9

# *It Takes Two*

## By Dan and Hallie Lord

---

### Hallie: The Ginger to His Fred

A few years ago a friend mentioned that her husband had surprised her with ballroom dancing classes for their anniversary. She was to be the Ginger to his Fred, she said. Now it's quite possible that I am the least graceful creature in all of God's kingdom, but upon hearing this news I immediately became convinced that I, too, wanted my own *Swing Time* moment.

"Why doesn't Dan want to dance with me?" I grumbled to my best friend, Jen. "I bet he's embarrassed by my two left feet. Do *you* think he's embarrassed by my two left feet?"

Jen assured me that he most definitely was not, to which I dramatically replied: "I just wish he was a little more romantic, that's all."

"Wait," Jen said incredulously. "Stop. Did you just say that you wish Dan was more romantic? The man who composes love songs for you? Have you lost your mind? And Hallie? I'm really sorry, but I'm just not sure that Dan is the ballroom-dancing type."

Touché. I can be something of a slow learner, but I assure you that was the last time I played the Comparison Game.

Even before Dan and I were twinkles in our fathers' eyes, and before our heavenly Father formed us in our mothers' wombs, he destined us for one another. Before all of time he willed that we would delight in one another. In spite of all our idiosyncrasies, peccadilloes, and weaknesses, he created us to be one another's solace amid the storm of our fallen world. How about that?

And yet, even with this knowledge, most of us are guilty of indulging in this fruitless exercise from time to time. Somehow the grass is always greener in someone else's yard. Oh, if only our husbands had such green thumbs, we lament.

But here's the thing: no man can be perfect in every way, but can your husband be perfect for you? God seems to think so, and word has it that he would know.

Perhaps it's true that Dan isn't likely to don tap shoes anytime soon, but does he tuck our sweet peas tightly into bed at night so that I can go to sleep early? Does he rise with the sun to go into work to provide for our family? Does he mop floors, scrub toilets, and fold laundry simply to ease my earthly burden?

And does he create songs that speak love to little, undeserving, and far too often ungrateful me?

Why yes, he does. Comparing my behind-the-scenes view of my marriage with another person's highlight reel has never brought anything other than discord and a lack of contentment. Counting my blessings, on the other hand, allows me to experience my marriage as the small taste of heaven that it's meant to be.

And when Dan swings me around our kitchen as our tiny olive shoots dance at our feet, I think, "Who could ask for anything more?"

Dan: Being Stupidly Open to Life

For me, before any of our children, before there was a Hallie in my life, and before it had occurred to me that anyone besides a few wizened clerics and my mom might want to actually *apply* what they had been told about Christianity, before all of that, there was music. I loved music.

All of my childhood years I had been quietly marinating in a musical sauce made of Henry Mancini, Peter Tchaikovsky, big band stuff, and the whole range of the American songbook. There are a lot of chefs in life's kitchen, though, and not all of them are culinarily competent. So my sauce absorbed a lot of Rick Springfield, Super Gold Light Rock Classics like "Crazy Love" by Poco, and everything by the Eagles. In fact, now that I think about it, this may have directly led to my alienation from God.

Regardless, I did experience a long period of separation from our Creator. At first it was because I had become enthralled with music. Later, though, it was because I became enthralled with myself and my desired pole position in the musical world. My band, Pain, and I plumbed the smoky depths of many a bar from Pensacola to New York to Chicago to San Diego, with a brief stop in Topeka, Kansas.

However, along the way to fulfilling my destiny as the Next Great Musical Genius, I was presented with two insurmountable problems: Hallie and God. Both of them challenged me to love someone besides myself, and with a love that involved humility, good behavior, and self-abnegation. Somehow that triple-threat formula works, as ridiculous as it may sound.

I have a personal theory that nobody can be a true child of God without becoming a father or mother. I don't care if you are a priest, a nun, gay, or if you were born without genitalia — if you are a human, God will call you to be a father or a mother to *someone*, helping that someone to grow in the light that you reflect from God, and in so doing *you* will become a more trusting, carefree child of the heavenly Father.

Of course, this is a theory (an admittedly abstract theory that I doubt will resonate with many people) that I've cooked up in *recent* years. At first, Hallie and I just wanted kids — we knew long before we got married that we did, and that we wanted hundreds of them, and that it would be just bucket-loads of fun.

"Morons," you may be thinking. Indeed, I fully acknowledge that is not the attitude modern people usually have when approaching marriage. Even the Church is very clear that although children are the "crowning glory"[29] of marriage, at the same time it recognizes the possibility that a married couple may have "serious motives to space out births."[30] But what can I say? It just never entered the collective mind of Hallie and me that the Church's qualification could possibly apply to us. After all, we were married, we were healthy, and we were nuts about each other. What possible reason could there be to delay children? Nary a one.

So, we bred. We bred like we were the last alien pod-people left alive on the planet of Sex.

There were many people in our lives who were not amused. I quickly realized this lack of amusement was everywhere. I remember taking a sociology class (having begun a regimen of night classes as part of my post-band return to college) in which the textbook took it for absolute granted that ancient societies had large families for one reason only: they were agrarian and needed help on the farm. Brilliant sociologists with doctorates had gotten together and simply decided this. As if there were stone tablets dug up somewhere confirming its veracity. As if two or three thousand years ago a husband came stumbling into the house sweating and panting from leading his yoked oxen through his wheat fields and said to his wife, "Whew! I am *beat*, woman! You need to start pumping out some kids so I can get a little help around here! No, it can't be just one or two! *Look at the size of these fields* ... I'm going to need eight ... no, nine ... awww, just make it *ten*."

But people don't have — and never have had — children to enlarge their workforce.

They have children because children make life *better*. It is indescribable joy just to see them come forth — they deserve to be here, and it's our honor and pleasure to be a part of it all. They fill up our lives and our hearts and teach us to love more than our selves. That's why people have children, Professor Anonymous Sociologist, not because they are in need of indentured servants or a private army.

Be open to life. You may never get to have children — but the likelihood is that you will. If you can have children, remember that it's only because God has made it so: he's given you the "equipment" to make it happen, the perfect helpmate with whom to share this vocation, and he will provide you with money, food, shelter, and everything that babies need.

Yes, of course it's all going to hurt. So what?

---

## Hallie: Drink Your Fill of Love

In the beginning, boy met girl, love blossomed, and romance filled our every waking moment. I'd spot a dress in a shop window and instantly wonder whether Dan would find it fetching. I'd cut pie recipes out of my *Cooks Illus-*

*trated* magazine; Dan likes pie so pies I'd bake. Nothing to do on a Saturday morning? We'd jump in the car and drive aimlessly until we found a shoreline, movie theater, or hidden treasure of a restaurant. Even the clouds in the sky reminded me of my guy.

Then came marriage and, two years later, the baby in the baby carriage. Our hearts doubled in size as we fell head over heels in love with the little boy who bore his father's name. We stood in awe as we slipped into the roles of mother and father and fell even more deeply in love.

But all that romance that had once come as easily as breathing? Well, it took a back seat. For a while this was well and good. Priorities are ever shifting, and at the start of family life it is natural that much of our energy would be oriented toward learning the ropes of parenthood. I poured myself out body and soul as I rocked and nursed and played with our sweet new baby, while Dan dutifully went out into the world to bring home the bacon.

Where did this leave our marriage? In many ways it was stronger than ever. We had come together and (with a little help from the Man upstairs) created an actual human being. What could be more bonding than that?

But in other ways, I began to feel slightly alienated from Dan. The romantic aspect of our union, which once imbued our every moment together, had suddenly gone missing. I didn't desire him any less, and I certainly hadn't fallen out of love with him, so I was left baffled as to why we didn't seem to be connecting the way we once had.

I'll spare you the histrionics that mildly melodramatic me had to wrestle with as I adjusted to this new reality. I'll simply say that, as with everything in life, our romantic life required a bit more thought and effort now that we had a baby on board.

We no longer had the freedom to hop in the car and head out to a dinner for two. Even the romantic rendez-vous of the more intimate variety suddenly had to be timed just right between the baby's second and third waking of the night.

But, you know, that's not such a bad thing. When you have to wait for that which you desire, those secret glad eyes, flirty text messages, and suggestive notes tucked into the pockets of briefcases come out to play. Spontaneity gets replaced with the most delicious anticipation. Truth be told, that's not a bad trade-off.

When overwhelmed by the duties of parenthood, it's easy to let the sexual-love aspect of your marriage slip a lit-tle. There are seasons of life when there's no getting around that, and so we grit our teeth and offer it up. What needs to be avoided, though, is downplaying the importance of spending quality time with your spouse.

That mothering instinct that would have you throw yourself in front of ongoing traffic for your child is the same instinct that might mistakenly (though understand-ably) prioritize your children over your husband. When you feel that temptation tap you on the shoulder and whis-per your name, try to remember this: your husband is your rock, and your marriage is the foundation that your entire family rests upon. Not only do you deserve the pleasure of romance, but the stability of your family demands that it get its due time.

So, bake that pie or buy that little gift, light the can-dles, give him an irresistible come-hither stare, whisper sweet nothings, and, "Eat, friends, drink; drink your fill of love!" (Song of Songs 5:1, NIV).

Dan: Tips for Not Being a Horrible Father

### 1. Set Your Face Like Flint

Men do not like the sensation of failing to be manly, the same as women do not like the sensation of failing to be womanly — both genders know deep down there are certain behaviors expected of them and they are not comfortable unless they are living up to those standards. When they do fail to live up to those standards, many men do a funny thing. Rather than stop the unmanly behavior, they choose the almost infinitely lazier option of pretending that the unmanly behavior *is* manly.

For instance, here's a shameful revelation from my own past, which I reveal only on the condition that you will not emulate me in any way.

Once, some years ago, we were hanging pictures. It was a Saturday afternoon, I believe. The weather was lovely, I had no real work to do, and Hallie and the three or so kids we had at the time (all under the age of four) and I were happily gathered in the living room just being together. A perfect little day.

We had not been living in that house long, so the walls were still bare and in need of decoration. From the remaining store of boxes in the garage, Hallie had pulled a watercolor painting of a potted Bougainvillea that my mom had done for us. The purple-red petals practically wagged in the breeze, set as they were upon an ivory canvas and in a frame as white as Gulf Coast beach sand. Hallie had decided it would look just right over the couch, and I dutifully responded with hammer and nails in hand.

The children toddled around the room. Hallie's smile sparkled. Light music played in the background, and only goodness and love would follow me all the days of my life....

Then I tripped over a baby. I can't remember which one — it must have been Sophia, who was still crawling. Actually, I didn't trip over her. As I held the painting of the Bougainvillea aloft and stepped back to see if I had it aligned right, I almost stepped on Sophia, but at the last possible nanosecond I realized she was underfoot and I sharply pulled my leg back up. This reaction caused me a kind of full-body spasm, and my arms reflexively yanked the painting in close, bringing the edge of the frame into contact with my left eyebrow with extreme prejudice.

Rather than taking this opportunity to practice some self-discipline and meekness, rather than "setting my face like flint" as Our Lord did and literally "take it like a man," what did I do? I shrieked in outrage. With wild eyes I kicked an object (not Sophia, thank goodness), I slammed a chair, I threw a pillow, I spewed obscenities, and I took the Lord's name in vain, all the while bleeding liberally upon the carpet and upon that beach-sand-white picture frame, and all in the presence of my stunned wife and children who were positively relying on me to be a model of manliness, not a maniacal hobgoblin.

Perversely, my subsequent reaction was not to say to my family: "I'm sorry ... I lost my mind for a moment." Instead, I circled wagons, assuring Hallie and myself that that is just how a guy is, how a guy gets mad, and that "peoples needs to be respectin' me."

But that was only compounding weakness with weakness, wasn't it? I had failed to live up to a good standard of manliness, but then I made it worse by pretending that the unmanly behavior *was* manly.

This poison can inform men's sexual lives, too. A man's worst traits and impulses can lead him to womanizing, but he will tell himself and other sympathetic men who are all trying to reinforce their own rotten behavior that womanizing is manly, and they will all laugh together and give each other high-fives and make animal noises like a bunch of chimpanzees in a jungle.

I remember once being encouraged by a coworker to cheat on my wife — he grudgingly acknowledged there was something vaguely admirable about my commitment to remain faithful, but warned me that it was important to "keep my skills up." See that? To make immorality legitimate, he had to tell himself that cheating was manly, requiring strength and extra effort and the maintaining of special "skills," and to do otherwise was to be weak and "unskilled."

To be meek, to be humble, to be chaste, to be patient: these require a far stronger, more durable, more reliable, more powerful man than the inclinations of the weak milquetoast who throws temper tantrums.

Set your faces like flint, men! The husband-and-father vocation is not for losers. If it helps, have your name legally changed to Flint.

## 2. Set Your Heart to Thaw

On the other hand, flintiness of face is not a license to be grim. If your nature is serious, sober, even solemn, that's perfectly fine; there are many rooms in our Father's house. But as an earthly father you have your work cut out for you, because your children are not meant to behave seriously, soberly, and solemnly very much of the time. Play with them. Let them play with you. Let them see what St. John of the Cross means when he writes, "The soul of the one who loves God always swims in joy, always keeps holiday, and is always in a mood for singing."[31]

I wish I could be more perspicuous, but when your children are all looking at you with their big, dewy eyes and they've built a tent out of your bed-sheets and furniture and invited you inside where there are slices of processed cheese and some Starbursts on a plastic plate with enough for you to share, it will all become very clear. Just go in and enjoy being a father. But check the cheese for strands of hair.

------

## Hallie: Refined by Fire

When I was younger, in the pink of health and relatively burden-free, pride and selfishness were my constant companions. I didn't know it at the time, of course, but they were. It's easy to deceive yourself when you have yet to truly be tested.

But time marches on, babies are born, bodies get weary, spirits carry the weight of the world, and we realize that maybe, just maybe, we can't do it all. Maybe we're not quite as strong as we thought. Maybe we need a little help.

This is not an easy lesson to learn, as it turns out, and one that I got a crash course in when I conceived our first child. Never could I have imagined the ways in which bringing Daniel into the world would bring me face to face with my own helplessness.

I felt helpless as I bent over in the bathroom wracked by nausea day after endless day. Helpless as I lumbered around in the third trimester with nine pounds of baby boy tucked inside me. Helpless as the contractions seemed to rip me in two. Helpless as I pushed him out into the world.

But I wasn't helpless. Christ was there. And so was Dan.

There have been times, too, when Dan needed me to carry him. Times when work sucked him dry of energy and cheer. Times when a lack of work weighed heavily on his spirit. I wish I could say I was the picture of grace and his constant source of comfort, but the death of selfishness is a long process. Perhaps, even, a lifelong one.

But through these trials, little by little, we both have been refined by fire.

Fire, I'm sure you'll agree, is the perfect metaphor, because regardless of the role you find yourself playing at any given moment, it's all hard. It's hard to be dependent, and it's hard to die to self when your spouse's needs overshadow your own.

But this is what marriage is all about: carrying one another and letting ourselves be carried, through life, to Christ, and finally to heaven.

If we can just learn to surrender, though, we will watch amazed as love reveals itself. The love of a husband caring for his wife, and vice versa; the love required to let someone see you at your worst and allow them to carry you; and the love of Christ who allows us to be his hands, feet, and heart.

I say "just," but it is perhaps these that are the most difficult of all earthly lessons to learn.

It's challenging to see your spouse dropping the ball and, rather than be angry because it doesn't seem fair, choose to make peace with the fact that sometimes God asks you to compensate and carry a heavier burden for a time.

It's hard to feel powerless and unable to contribute more to your marriage and have to learn that though all husbands and wives are called to be continually giving 100 percent, sometimes your 100 percent is going to look a lot smaller than your spouse's.

It's painful to feel your knees buckle under the weight of it all and hear God ask you for more — to give more, lean on him more, and accept more suffering, pain, and grace.

These things, though, are the wrecking balls that break down our walls of selfishness and pride.

And let me tell you, dear friends, when those walls start to crumble and Christ's light pushes through the cracks, you will grab your spouse, kiss those lips, and thank God for all that miserable suffering. Every last bit of it.

---

*Dan Lord is the author of* Choosing Joy: The Secret to Living a Fully Christian Life. *He currently teaches theology, writes for various publications, and is the advisory editor for Catholic Exchange. Hallie Lord is the editor of* Style, Sex, and Substance: 10 Catholic Women Consider the Things That Really Matter, *and she blogs at www.moxiewife.com. Dan and Hallie live with their children in South Carolina.*

# Notes

1     For a fuller discussion of temperament and its role in marriage, see our book *The Temperament God Gave Your Spouse.*

2     John Gottman, Ph.D., Julie Schwartz Gottman, Ph.D., *Ten Lessons to Transform Your Marriage* (New York: Crown Publishers, 2006).

3     St. John Chrysostom, *On Marriage and Family Life* (Yonkers, NY: St. Vladimir's Seminary Press, 1986).

4     *The Nature and Mission of Theology* (San Francisco: Ignatius Press, 1995), 32–33.

5     Corrie ten Boom, *The Hiding Place* (New York: Bantam Books, 1971), 238.

6     U.S. Bureau of the Census, 2005–2009 American Community Survey 5-Year Estimates. Calculations by David Lapp, September 5, 2013.

7     David Lapp, "Did I Get Married Too Young?" *The Wall Street Journal*, February 11, 2010, accessed September 9, 2013, online.wsj.com/article/SB10001424052748704107204575039150739864666.html.

8     Kay Hymowitz, Jason S. Carroll, W. Bradford Wilcox, and Kelleen Kaye, *Knot Yet: The Benefits and Costs of Delayed Marriage in America* (The National Marriage Project at the University of Virginia, The National Campaign to Prevent Teen and Unplanned Pregnancy, and The Relate Institute, 2013), 20.

9     Ibid., 14–16.

10    William J. Doherty, "Take Back Your Marriage: A Challenge to Couples, Congregations, and Communities" (keynote presentation at the annual meeting of Smart Marriages, Orlando, Florida, June 21, 2001), accessed September 14, 2013, www.smartmarriages.com/citizen.marriage.html.

11    Barry Schwartz, *The Paradox of Choice: Why More Is Less* (New York: Harper Perennial, 2004).

12    Wendell Berry, "Renewing Husbandry," *Orion Magazine*, September/October 2005, accessed September 9, 2013, www .orionmagazine.org/index.php/articles/article/160/.

13    Ina May Gaskin, *Ina May's Guide to Breastfeeding* (New York: Bantam, 2009), 60–61.

14    Karol Wojtyla, *Love and Responsibility*, trans. H.T. Willetts, rev. ed. (1981; repr., San Francisco: Ignatius Press, 1993), 126.

15    W. Bradford Wilcox and Elizabeth Marquardt, *The State of Our Unions: When Baby Makes Three — How Parenthood Makes Life Meaningful and How Marriage Makes Parenthood Bearable* (The National Marriage Project and the Institute for American Values, 2011), 40–44.

16    Dean M. Busby, Jason S. Carroll, and Brian J. Willoughby, "Compatibility or Restraint: The Effects of Sexual Timing on Marriage Relationships," *Journal of Family Psychology* 24, no. 6 (December 2010), 766–774.

17    Wilcox & Marquardt, *The State of Our Unions*, 31–33.

18    We are grateful to Bill Doherty for this insight.

19    St. Josemaría Escrivá, *The Way; Furrow; The Forge* (New York: Scepter, 2008), 746.

20    www.cdc.gov/nchs/data/nhsr/nhsr049.pdf

21    www.nytimes.com/2012/04/15/opinion/sunday/the-downside- of-cohabiting-before-marriage.html?pagewanted=all&_r=0

22    www.cdc.gov/nchs/data/nhsr/nhsr049.pdf

23    stateofourunions.org/2011/SOOU2011.php

24    verilymag.com/moving-in-what-i-know-now/

25    www.nytimes.com/2012/04/15/opinion/sunday/the-downside- of-cohabiting-before-marriage.html?pagewanted=all&_r=0

26    www.rand.org/content/dam/rand/pubs/working_papers/ WR1000/WR1001/RAND_WR1001.pdf

27    www.nytimes.com/2012/04/15/opinion/sunday/the-downside- of-cohabiting-before-marriage.html?pagewanted=all&_r=0

28    www.healthymarriageinfo.org/research-and-policy/marriage-facts/national/index.aspx

29    Bl. Pope Paul VI, *Gaudium et Spes*, 48.

30    Bl. Pope Paul VI, *Humanae Vitae*, 16.

31    Butler, Alban. *The Lives of the Fathers, Martyrs, and Other Principal Saints* (New York: P.J. Kennedy, 1902), Vol. XI.